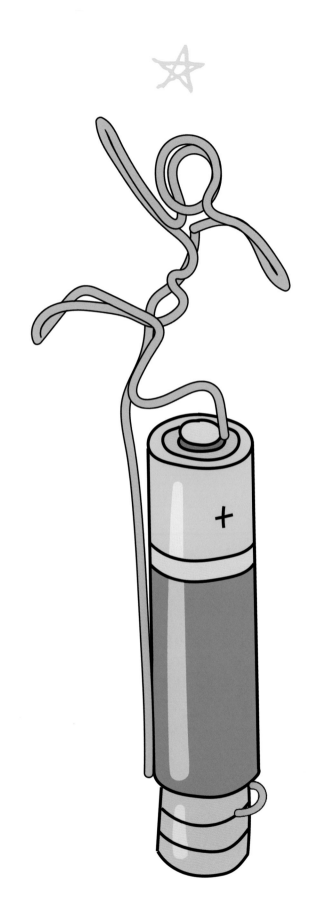

sensational Science

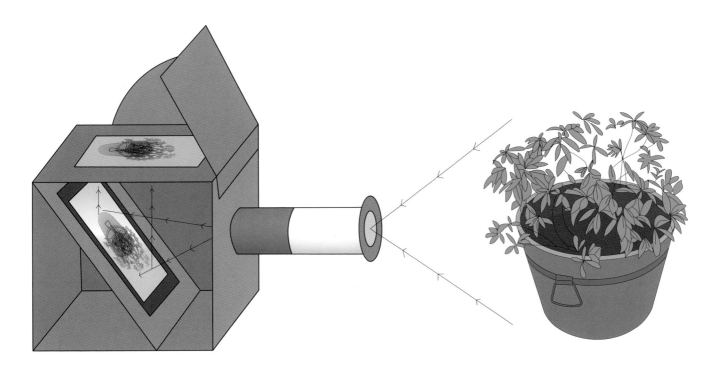

by Rob Ives
Illustrated by Eva Sassin

Contents

Beetle Books and Hungry Banana are imprints of Hungry Tomato Ltd

US Edition (Beetle Books)
ISBN 978 1 913077 143

UK Edition (Hungry Banana)
ISBN 978 1 913077 242

First published in 2019
by Hungry Tomato Ltd
Old Bakery Studios, Blewetts Wharf
Malpas Road, Truro, TR1 1JQ, UK
Copyright © 2019 Hungry Tomato Ltd

A CIP catalog record for this book is available from the British Library.

Printed and bound in the USA

Discover more at
www.mybeetlebooks.com
www.hungrytomato.com

Sensational Science

Science is fun, amazing, and full of wonder. Dip in and discover a world of scientific activities. Create homemade lightning, discover how magnets work, make your own periscope to see over a wall or a simple hovercraft, and much, much, more. All you need are simple household items, to try out these brilliant experiments. Get ready, Sensational Science starts here!

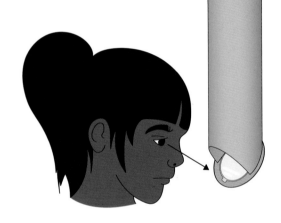

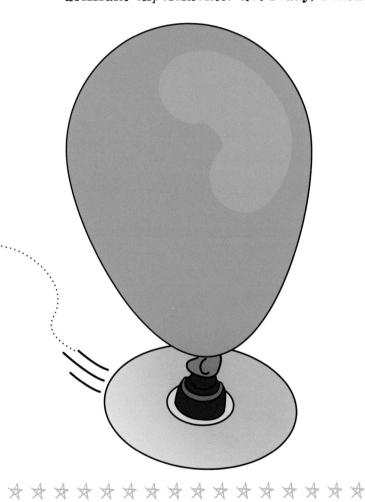

Watch for this sign throughout the book. You may need help from an adult to complete these experiments.

Safety First

Take care and use good sense with these amazing science experiments— some are very simple, while others are trickier.

Each project includes a list of everything you will need. Most of the items are things you can find around the house, or they are things that are readily available and inexpensive to buy.

Be sure to check out the Amazing Science behind the projects and learn the scientific principles involved in each experiment.

Electricity

Did you know that even though electricity is one of the basic forces in the universe, scientists only really discovered it a few centuries ago? And when they did, they thought electricity was so amazing, that it must be what makes us alive? That's why, in the movies, Frankenstein's monster was brought to life with a zap of lightning—natural electricity. Now you can make your very own mini lightning flash and ten other fun projects sparked by electricity.

You'll see how to turn a toothbrush into a robot, how to make a magnet you can switch on and off, and how to make a flashlight to light your way. You'll even discover how to make your own electricity! Prepare to charge!

You will need

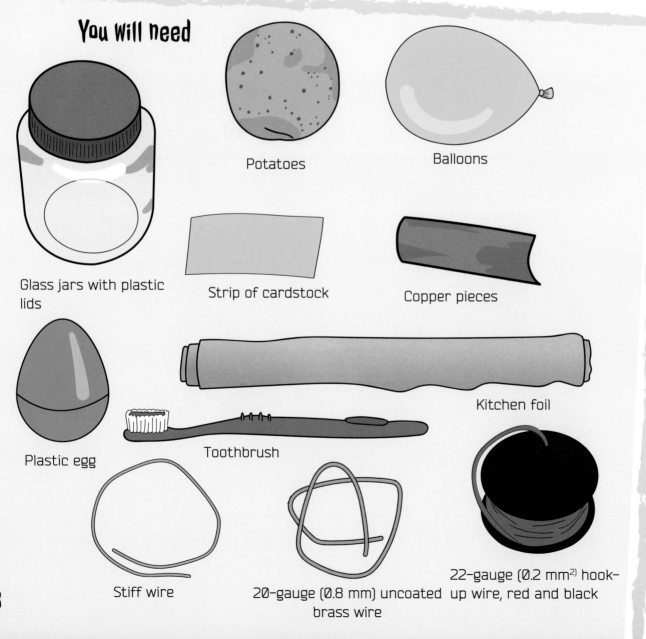

Glass jars with plastic lids

Potatoes

Balloons

Strip of cardstock

Copper pieces

Plastic egg

Toothbrush

Kitchen foil

Stiff wire

20-gauge (0.8 mm) uncoated brass wire

22-gauge (0.2 mm²) hook-up wire, red and black

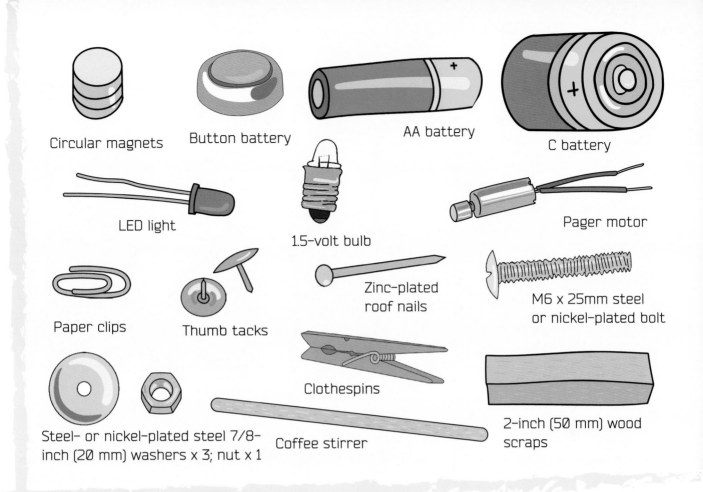

Circular magnets

Button battery

AA battery

C battery

LED light

1.5-volt bulb

Pager motor

Paper clips

Thumb tacks

Zinc-plated roof nails

M6 x 25mm steel or nickel-plated bolt

Steel- or nickel-plated steel 7/8-inch (20 mm) washers x 3; nut x 1

Clothespins

Coffee stirrer

2-inch (50 mm) wood scraps

What Tools Will I Need?

Sticky Tack

Double-sided sticky foam pads

Clear tape

Gaffer tape (or duct tape)

Electrical tape

Scissors

Long-nose pliers

Voltage meter (available online)

Craft utility knife

Junior hacksaw

Homopolar Motor

A homopolar motor is a super simple electric motor with only one moving part—in this case, the wire. One end has to touch the battery's positive terminal. The other end touches the magnet.

You Will need

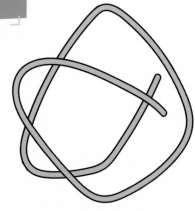

Three circular magnets, roughly the diameter of the battery

Non-magnetic wire, such as 20-guage (0.8 mm) uncoated brass wire

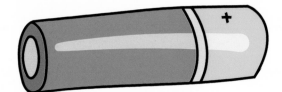

AA battery

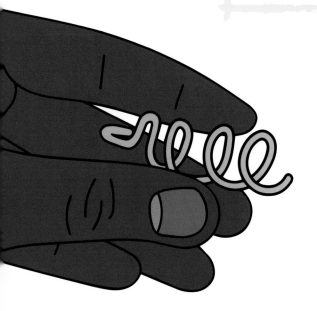

1. Coil the wire so that it fits loosely around the battery. Double one end over in a hook shape.

2. Stand the battery on the magnets. Now you'll need to reshape the wire. The hooked end rests on the top of the battery, the coil hangs loosely around the battery, and the other end of the wire must gently touch the magnets at the bottom. Once you have it just right, the wire will spin around the battery with surprising enthusiasm!

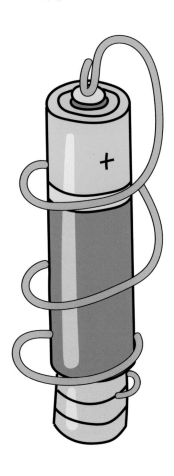

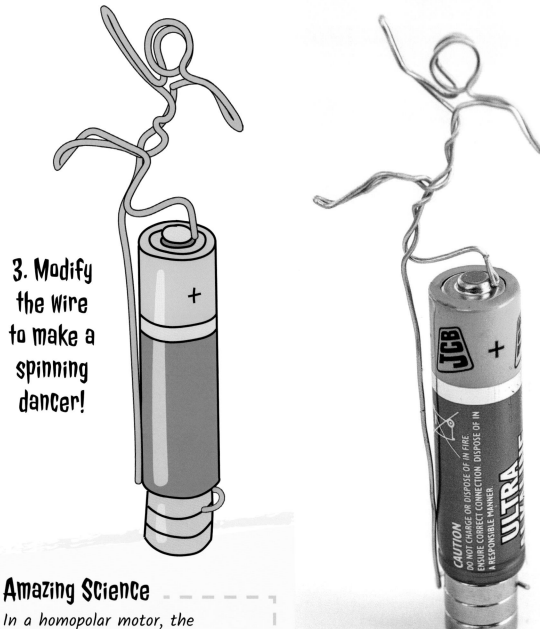

3. Modify the wire to make a spinning dancer!

Amazing Science

In a homopolar motor, the current running through the wire generates a magnetic field (area of magnetism) which makes a magnet move—similar to the more complicated electric motor on the right. In this project, the field is at a right angle to the field of the disc magnet, so they push against each other to make the wire rotate.

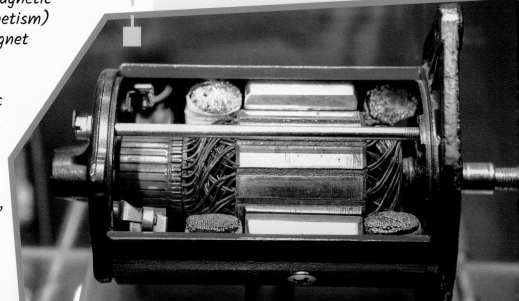

Brush Bot

The brush bot is a tiny robot powered by a tiny electric motor. Turn on the bot and it will scoot round any smooth surface with surprising speed and in surprising directions!

You Will need

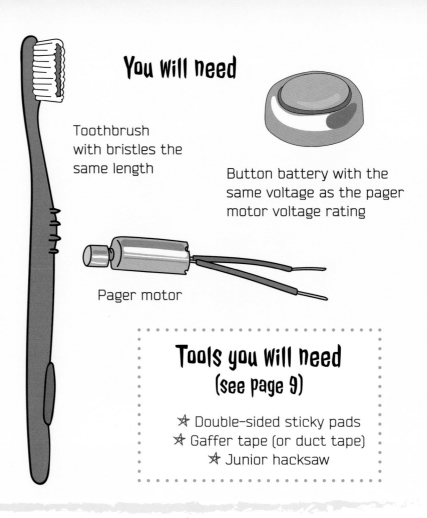

Toothbrush with bristles the same length

Button battery with the same voltage as the pager motor voltage rating

Pager motor

Tools you Will need
(see page 9)

✭ Double-sided sticky pads
✭ Gaffer tape (or duct tape)
✭ Junior hacksaw

1. Cut the head off the toothbrush with the hacksaw and discard the handle.

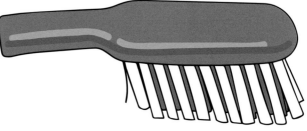

2. Squish the toothbrush down so that the bristles bend in one direction.

3. The bristles should look something like this—all slightly angled in the same direction.

4. A small pager motor will power the bot and can be bought online inexpensively.

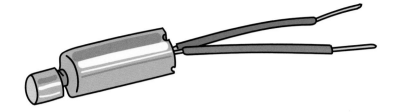

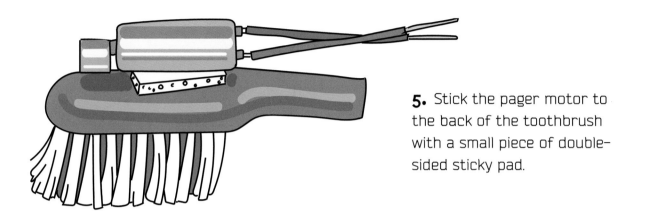

5. Stick the pager motor to the back of the toothbrush with a small piece of double-sided sticky pad.

6. Stick the battery to the neck of the toothbrush with another piece of sticky pad. Insert the red wire between the battery and the pad. The blue wire will get taped to the bottom of the battery.

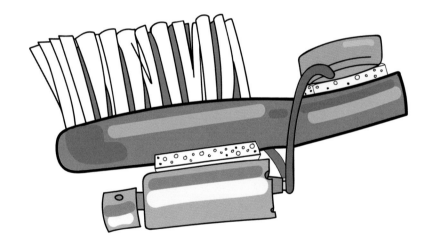

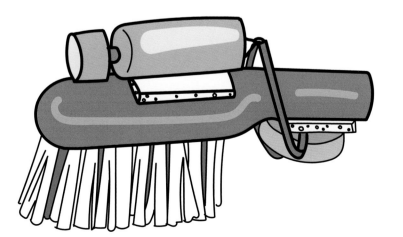

7. Ready for action! Tape the blue wire to the bottom of the battery and watch the robot go!

8. Make more than one color bot and race them!

Amazing Science

When English scientist Michael Faraday found that an electric current drives a magnet around and around, he showed how to make an electric motor. Here, the pager motor spins and sets up a vibration in the brush bot. As the bot vibrates, a ratchet effect pushes it backwards.

Faraday – Electricity

Mini Lightning

Real lightning is caused by the build-up of static electricity in clouds. This small-scale version uses static electricity from a balloon. It is stored between two layers of aluminum foil in a charge storer called a Leyden jar.

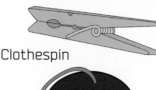

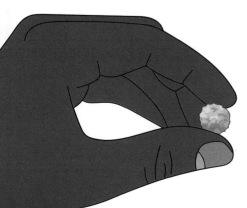

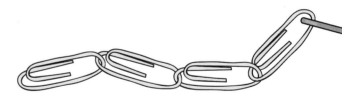

1. Carefully make a small hole in the plastic lid with the point of a craft knife to just fit the stiff wire.

2. Make a loop at the end of the stiff wire. Add a chain of paper clips.

3. Squish a piece of foil into a ball as smooth as possible.

4. Push the wire through the lid, and fit the straight end into the foil ball.

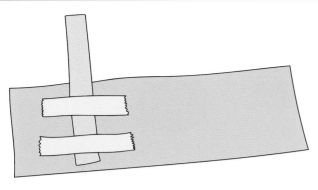

5. Cut two strips of foil that will cover the outside of the jar plus a little extra for overlap. Cut two smaller strips to use for tabs. Use clear tape to attach each smaller tab near the end of each foil.

6. Line the jar with a foil strip, with the tab lying across the bottom.

7. Wrap the second foil strip round the outside of the jar. Again, the tab should be at the bottom.

8. Fit the lid on the jar. The paper clip chain should connect the wire to the inner foil tab. The Leyden jar is now complete.

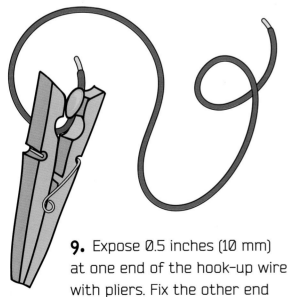

9. Expose 0.5 inches (10 mm) at one end of the hook-up wire with pliers. Fix the other end to the clothespin with a thumb tack. Clip it to the outer foil tab on the jar.

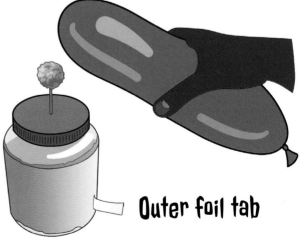

Outer foil tab

10. Charge up the Leyden jar by repeatedly rubbing an inflated balloon on your hair, then touching the balloon to the foil ball at the top of the wire. This transfers the static electricity into the jar.

16

11. Once the jar is charged, bring the end of the flying wire close to the ball and watch the fat spark jump between them. That's the electricity discharging or...

Lightning!

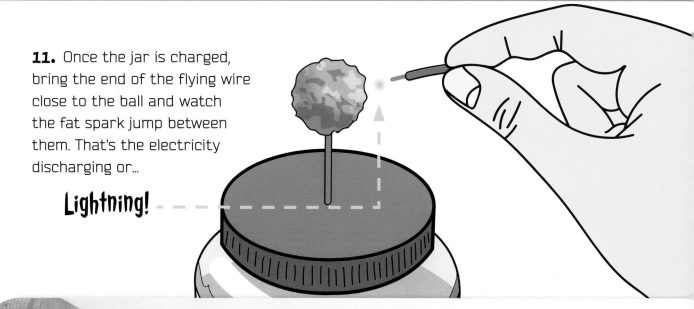

Amazing Science

Static electricity is electrically charged particles piled up in one place. Lightning starts when a massive amount of electrical charge slowly builds—then suddenly discharges (flows back) in one big flash.

17

Battery Flashlight

C battery

Sticky tack

Thumb tacks

2.5 inches (60 mm) 22-gauge (0.2 mm2) insulated hook-up wire, red and black x2

Imagine what it was like in the past when there were only candles to light up the long winter nights! These days we have electricity and bulbs—and we can make this flashlight! Use pliers to expose all the wire ends.

Half a plastic egg or a single section from an egg box for the reflector

Paper clip

2-inch-long (50 mm) wood scrap

Tools you will need (see page 9)

★ Long-nose pliers
★ Gaffer tape (or duct tape)
★ Craft utility knife

1.5-volt bulb

1. Make a hole with the utility knife in the bottom of the egg to fit the bulb. Expose the ends of one wire. Twist one end tightly around the bulb. Fit the bulb in place.

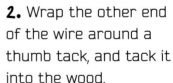

2. Wrap the other end of the wire around a thumb tack, and tack it into the wood.

3. Strip the ends of the other wire. Fix the paper clip and one end of the wire to the wood with a thumb tack. The paper clip must not touch the other thumb tack unless it is pressed.

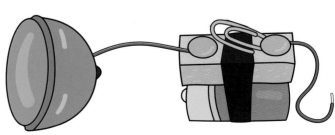

4. Tape the paper clip switch to the battery.

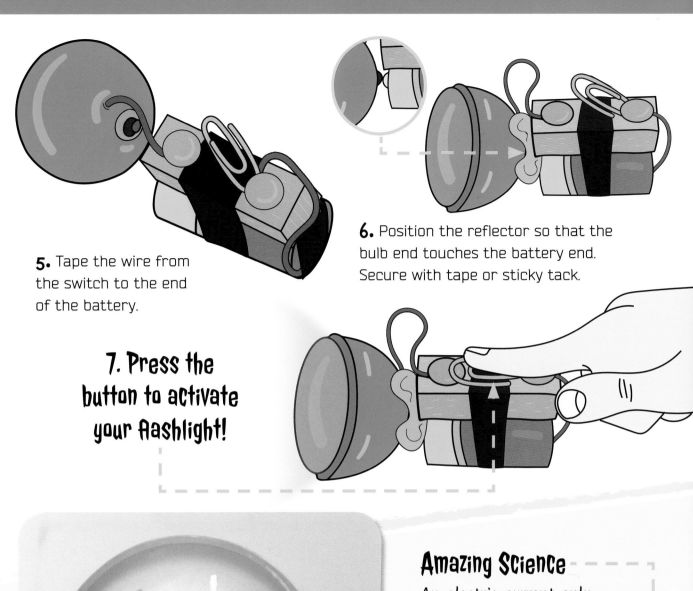

5. Tape the wire from the switch to the end of the battery.

6. Position the reflector so that the bulb end touches the battery end. Secure with tape or sticky tack.

7. Press the button to activate your flashlight!

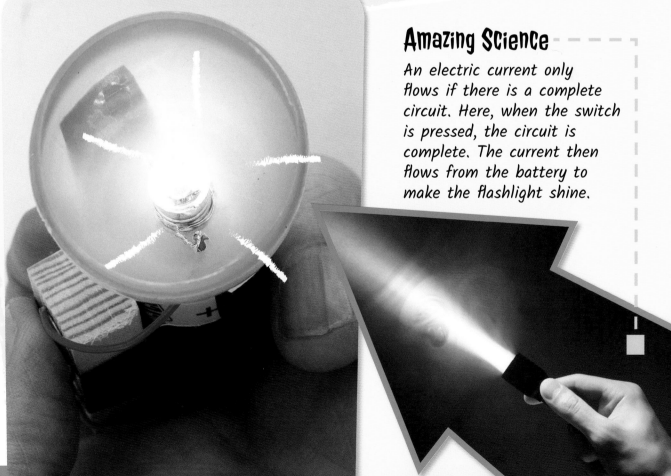

Amazing Science

An electric current only flows if there is a complete circuit. Here, when the switch is pressed, the circuit is complete. The current then flows from the battery to make the flashlight shine.

Electromagnet

An electromagnet works when the electricity is turned on. This electromagnet uses a battery to generate a magnetic field. Expose all wire ends by an inch (10 mm) before conecting to the battery.

22-gauge (0.2 mm2) insulated hook-up wire, red

Strip of cardstock

Wood scrap

1/4 x 1 inch (M6 x 25 mm) bolt, steel or nickel-plated steel

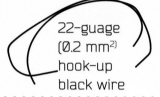

C battery

Two 7/8-inch (20 mm) washers and a 1/4-inch (M6) nut, steel or nickel-plated steel

Thumb tacks

Paper clip

22-guage (0.2 mm²) hook-up black wire

Tools you will need
(see page 9)

* Clear tape   * Electrical tape
* Gaffer tape   * Long-nose pliers

1. Cut the cardstock to the length of the bolt. Make it into a cylinder. Add one washer to the bolt, add the cylinder, add the second washer and bolt to fasten (see above). This is your magnetic core.

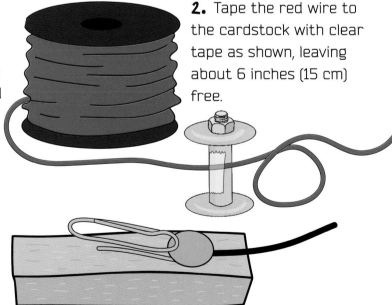

2. Tape the red wire to the cardstock with clear tape as shown, leaving about 6 inches (15 cm) free.

3. Wrap the wire tightly and evenly around the core and secure with tape. This is your electromagnet

4. For the switch, pin the paper clip to the wood while connecting it to 6 inches (15 cm) of black wire.

6. Connect a 6-inch (15 cm) length of black wire under a second thumb tack. The paper clip must only touch the second thumb tack when pressed down (*right*).

7. Using the gaffer tape, secure the wires from the electromagnet, and switch to the battery. Join the wire ends with electrical tape as shown.

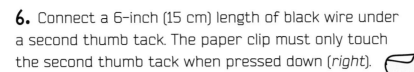

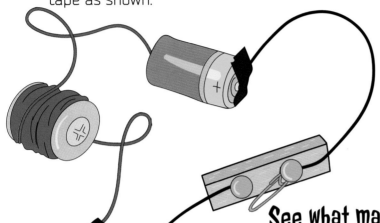

8. The circuit is ready! Press the switch to turn on the electromagnet.

See what materials the electromagnet will attract!

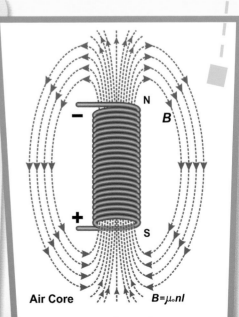

Amazing Science

An electric current creates its own magnetic field. Here, the bolt concentrates the wire's magnetic field. It is strengthened further each time the wire is wrapped around the bolt. This is why electromagnets can be very strong.

Air Core $B = \mu_o nI$

N

B

−

+

S

Telegraph

Before radio and telephones existed, the fastest way to communicate long-distance was by telegraph. The telegraph operator tapped a message in Morse code on the switch, and the receiver translated the clicks back into the message. You can try sending a message to another room. To do this, splice in two 10-foot (3 m) lengths of wire to your original circuit, one on either side, by twisting the exposed ends together. Tape the joins.

You Will need

Make the pushbutton switch and electromagnet coil on pages 20-21. Expose the ends of the wires by 1/3 inch (10 mm) before connecting them.

7/8-inch (20 mm) steel washer

Coffee stirrer, cut to 2.7 inches (70 mm)

2-inch-long (50 mm) wood scraps x2

0.2mm² hook-up wire (for a long-distance telegraph!)

Tools you Will need
(see page 9)

✯ Sticky foam pads
✯ Gaffer tape
✯ Electrical tape
✯ Epoxy glue
✯ Junior hacksaw

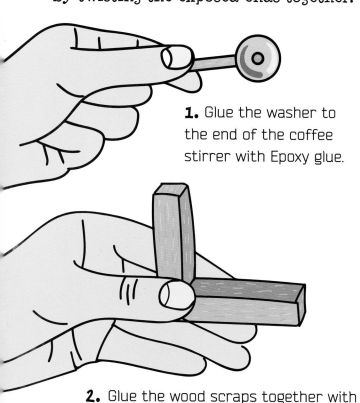

1. Glue the washer to the end of the coffee stirrer with Epoxy glue.

2. Glue the wood scraps together with white glue to make a frame.

3. Use sticky foam pads to stick the electromagnet coil to the frame. Use thumb tacks to fit the washer assembly into position so that it is just above the bolt.

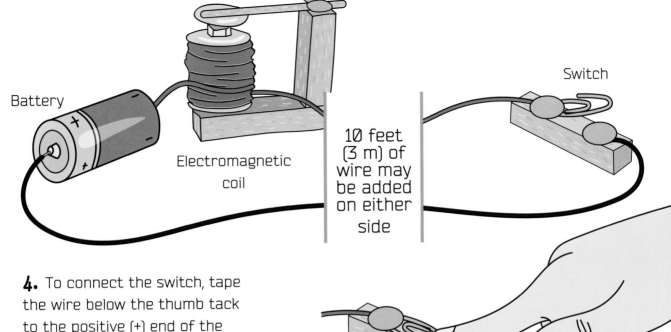

Battery

Electromagnetic coil

Switch

10 feet (3 m) of wire may be added on either side

4. To connect the switch, tape the wire below the thumb tack to the positive (+) end of the battery. Twist the bare ends of the other wire to one wire from the coil and cover with electrical tape. Tape the other coil wire to the other end of the battery.

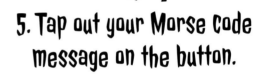

5. Tap out your Morse Code message on the button.

It will be received as clicks on the telegraph.

Amazing Science

The telegraph works by switching on a current as each letter is tapped. As you tap on your telegraph, electricity flows down the wire into the electromagnet. It attracts the metal washer to make the long and short clicks.

Charge Power

There are many ways a static electrical charge can build up, but how do you detect it? The answer is with an electroscope made from a few household items.

You will need

Large jar

Plastic lid to fit or cover the jar

Sticky tack

Two aluminum foil pieces, 1.5 x 0.4 inches (40 x 10 mm)

20-guage (0.8 mm) uncoated brass wire

Tools you will need
(see page 9)

★ Balloon
★ Craft utility knife

1. Use a piece of wire about the length of the jar. Make a coil in the top and a small hook at the other end.

2. Make a hole in the plastic lid with a craft knife. Thread the wire through and secure it with sticky tack.

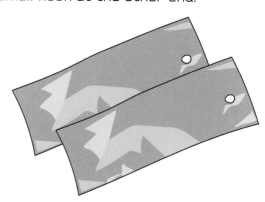

3. At one end of the two foil pieces, make a small hole just big enough for the wire.

4. Hang both pieces of foil from the wire.

5. Fit the lid to the jar with the foil strips inside. The foil must not touch the sides of the jar.

6. Your electroscope is complete!

Charge up a balloon by rubbing it on your hair, then bring it close to the wire spiral. The foil strips will move apart, showing the presence of electricity.

Amazing Science

In this electroscope, the amount the foil strips move apart indicates how much repulsion there is between like charges. The farther apart the foil strips, the greater the strength of the static electrical charge.

Potato Power

Did you know that you can power a light with electricity from a potato? Here's how...

You will need

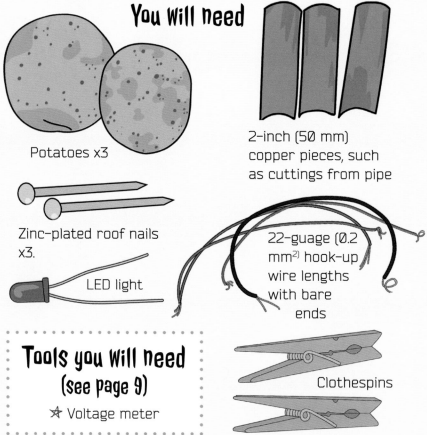

Potatoes x3

2-inch (50 mm) copper pieces, such as cuttings from pipe

Zinc-plated roof nails x3.

LED light

22-guage (0.2 mm²) hook-up wire lengths with bare ends

Clothespins

Tools you will need
(see page 9)

⭐ Voltage meter

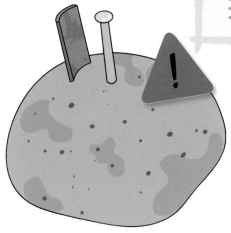

1. Push your zinc and copper pieces into a potato close together but not touching.

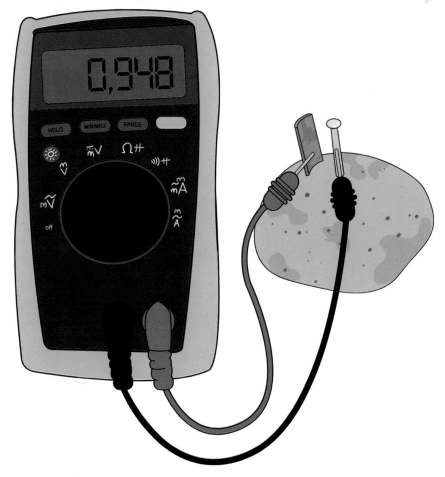

2. With a voltage meter you will be able to measure the electricity being generated by the potato.

3. Use four 4-inch (100 mm) lengths of wire and clothespins to connect three potatoes in series. Connect the zinc on one to the copper on the next and so on.

The two extreme ends can then be used to light your LED!

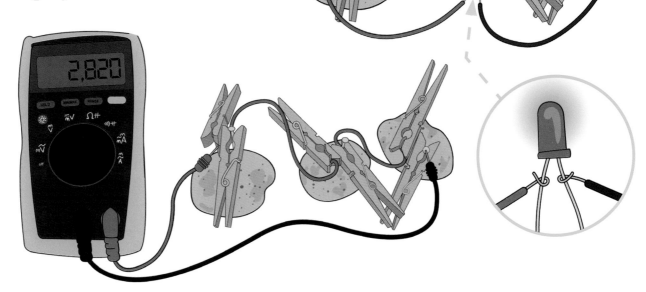

4. Check out the voltage on those taters!

Amazing Science

All you need to make an electric battery is two different metals: one for the anode (positive terminal), the other for the cathode (negative). You also need a substance called an electrolyte. This can even be a potato, which produces enough electricity to light an LED.

Forces and Motion

Forces are at the heart of everything that happens. A force is basically a push or a pull. It makes things accelerate—that is, change speed or direction. Without forces, nothing would ever happen because all things have natural inertia. This means they stay stock still until they are forced into moving! Things fall because of the force of gravity. You pick up a drink using the force of your muscles.

Discover how to use forces to create motion and blast a rocket into the air, power a superfast dragster, lift a hovercraft, and much more. May the force be with you!

You will need

Thumb tacks

Balloons

7/8-inch (25 mm) steel washers x 2

Liquid soap

Long, thin household candle

Craft sticks

Large and small paper clips

talcum powder

Talcum powder (baby powder)

Shallow tray

Thin craft foam

Drinks bottles with sports caps

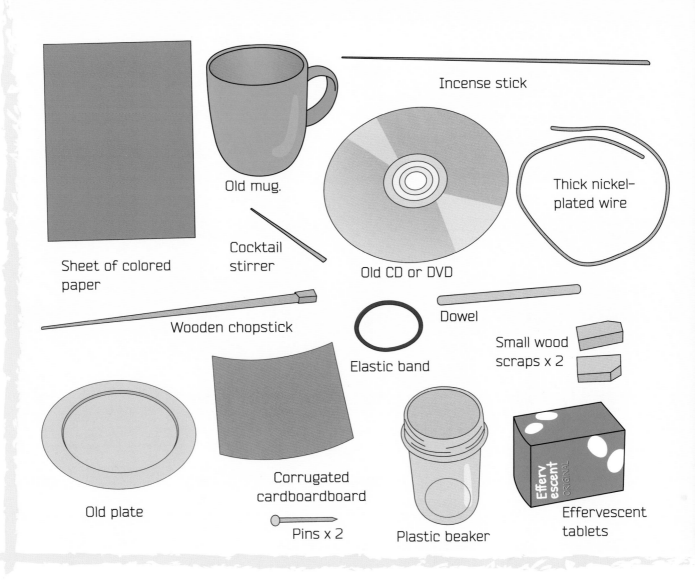

Sheet of colored paper

Old mug.

Cocktail stirrer

Incense stick

Old CD or DVD

Thick nickel-plated wire

Wooden chopstick

Dowel

Small wood scraps x 2

Elastic band

Old plate

Corrugated cardboardboard

Plastic beaker

Effervescent tablets

Pins x 2

What tools will I need?

Pencil

Gaffer tape

Small clamps or clothespins

White Glue

EPOXY

Epoxy Glue

Compass

Scissors

Craft utility knife

Craft drill

Lighter

Pliers

Side cutters

Bottle Rocket

A normal drink bottle turns into a mini rocket if it has enough propulsion. It may not land on the moon, but you'll be surprised at the whizzing power of fizz. So it's probably best to try this outside—in fact, DO try this outside!

You will need

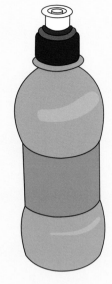

Drinks bottle with sports cap

Effervescent tablets x4

Old mug

1. Have four tablets ready to use.

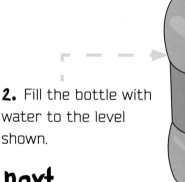

2. Fill the bottle with water to the level shown.

Complete these next steps as quickly as possible!

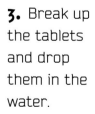

3. Break up the tablets and drop them in the water.

4. With the sports cap pressed down to close it, screw the lid on tight.

30

5. Shake the bottle a couple of times.

6. Place the bottle upside down in an old mug.

7. **Step back!**

8. The pressure from the tablets builds up, and when it gets high enough, it blows off the lid, launching the rocket out of the mug and skywards!

Amazing Science

Rockets blast through space by burning fuel to make rapidly expanding gases. The push, or reaction between the rocket and the gases drives the rocket forward. Here, the expanding gases from the indigestion tablets force water out through the nozzle, giving lift-off.

Balloon Hovercraft

A hovercraft is a clever form of transport that moves along on a cushion of air, so it doesn't touch the surface below. This allows it to travel over ice and land as well as water.

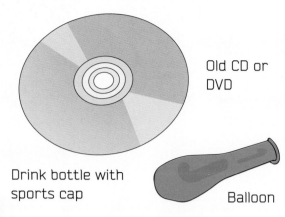
Old CD or DVD

Drink bottle with sports cap

Balloon

Tools you will need
(see page 29)

✷ Epoxy glue

1. Use Epoxy to glue the lid of the bottle over the hole in the CD.

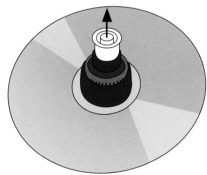

2. Pull up the sports cap so that air can flow freely through it.

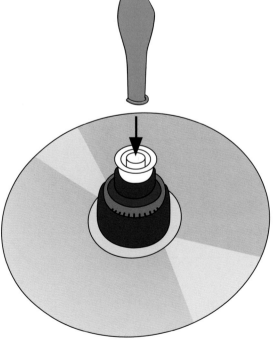

3. Fit the balloon over the lip of the sports cap.

32

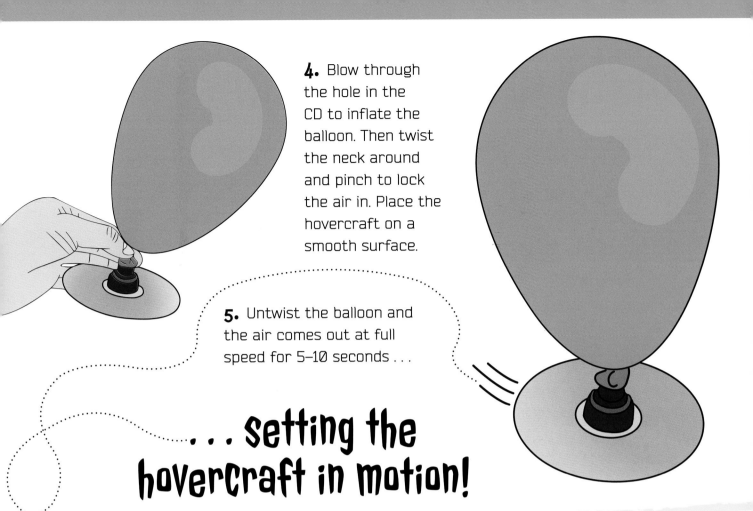

4. Blow through the hole in the CD to inflate the balloon. Then twist the neck around and pinch to lock the air in. Place the hovercraft on a smooth surface.

5. Untwist the balloon and the air comes out at full speed for 5–10 seconds . . .

. . . setting the hovercraft in motion!

Amazing Science

The air beneath a hovercraft is squeezed so that its push, or pressure, lifts the craft, letting it float over most surfaces. Here, the pressure of air outside squeezes the air inside the balloon out under the disc, so the disc floats like a hovercraft.

Elastic-band Dragster

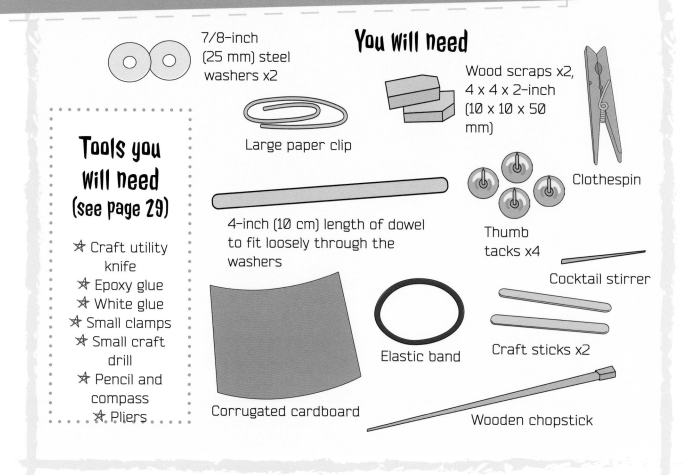

7/8-inch (25 mm) steel washers x2

You will need

Large paper clip

Wood scraps x2, 4 x 4 x 2-inch (10 x 10 x 50 mm)

Clothespin

4-inch (10 cm) length of dowel to fit loosely through the washers

Thumb tacks x4

Cocktail stirrer

Elastic band

Craft sticks x2

Corrugated cardboard

Wooden chopstick

Tools you will need (see page 29)

⚝ Craft utility knife
⚝ Epoxy glue
⚝ White glue
⚝ Small clamps
⚝ Small craft drill
⚝ Pencil and compass
⚝ Pliers

Dragsters are cars that accelerate very rapidly. They burn rocket fuel to release its energy and provide the force to send the dragster whizzing away!

1. Use a craft knife to shave off a diagonal from one corner of each wood scrap. This will make room for the elastic band. Fix the scraps to the chopstick with epoxy glue and clamp them as it dries.

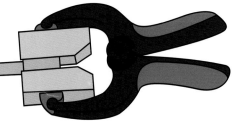

2. Use epoxy glue and thumb tacks to fix and pin the washers to the blocks, with the dowel threaded into place for the axle.

Thumb tack

3 in (80 mm)

1.5 in (40 mm)

Glue the two circles of cardboard together.

3. Use a pencil and compass and a craft knife to cut out four card circles: two 3-inch (2 x 80 mm), two 1.5-inch (2 x 40 mm).. Make them into the two large back wheels as shown, using white glue.

2 in (50 mm)

4. Make the front wheel the same way with two 2-inch (50 mm) circles of card. Pierce a small hole in the center to fit the cocktail stirrer through as the axle.

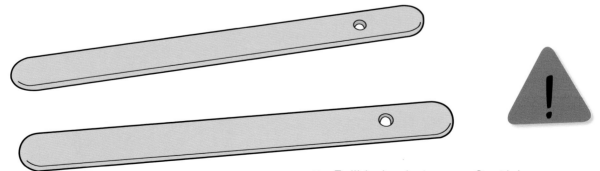

5. Drill holes in two craft sticks so that the front wheel axle is a loose fit.

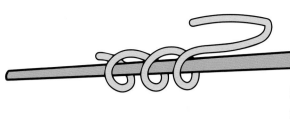

6. Use pliers to help you unfold the paper clip and make a wire to coil fairly loosely around the end of the chopstick. Keep a hook at the end.

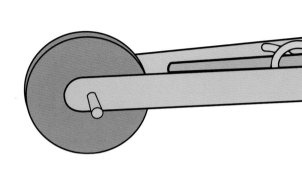

7. Fit on the front wheel and glue the craft sticks to the chopstick with white glue.

Cut open an elastic band and tie it to the wire hook.

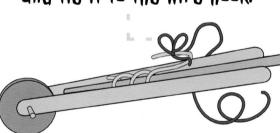

8. Pin and glue the wheels to the rear axle with a thumb tack at each end of the dowel and white glue.

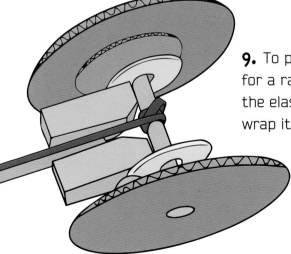

9. To prepare the car for a race, stretch out the elastic band and wrap it around the axle.

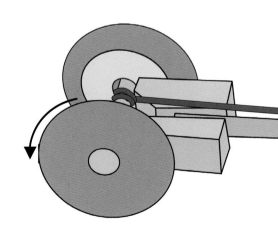

10. Turn the wheels backwards to stretch the elastic band and create the tension for it to race away.

11. A clothespin can be used to hold the car ready for launch.

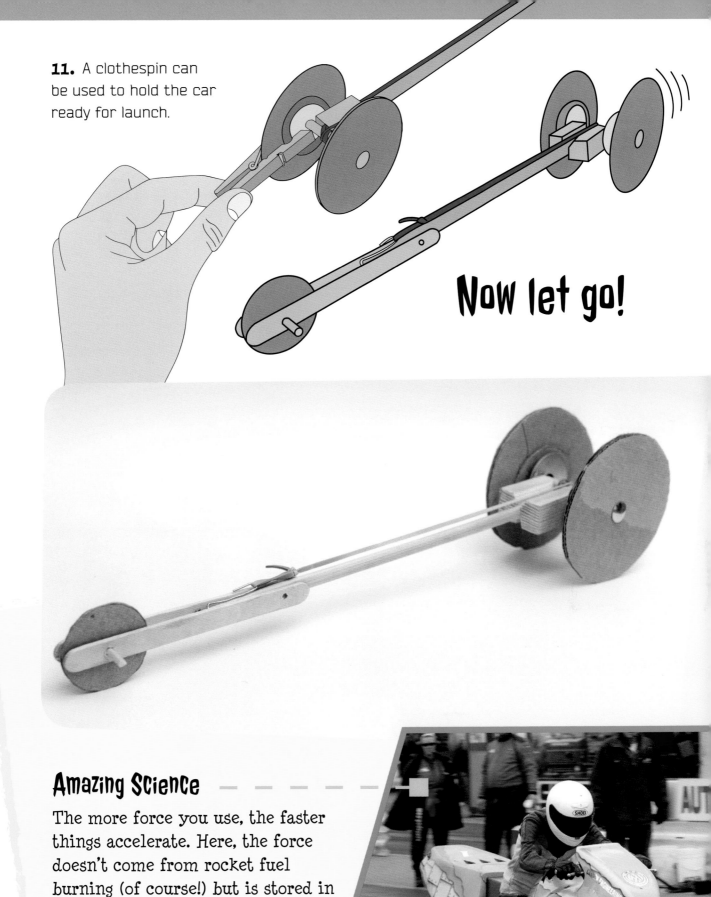

Now let go!

Amazing Science

The more force you use, the faster things accelerate. Here, the force doesn't come from rocket fuel burning (of course!) but is stored in the stretch of the elastic band. But the principle is the same.

Paper Plane

This paper aircraft is a fantastic little flyer. Just keep your lines straight, and points and creases sharp!

Single sheet of printer paper

Small paper clip

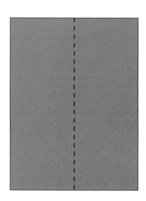

1. Fold the paper in half lengthwise, then open it out.

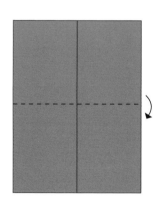

2. Fold it in half along the width. Keep this fold and fold along the previous crease, so it's folded into quarters.

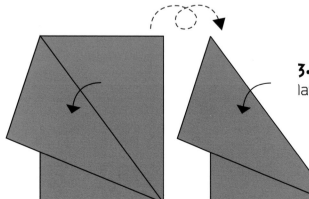

3. On both sides, fold back the two layers of paper along the diagonal.

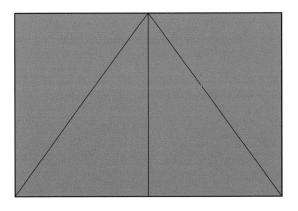

4. Open out the paper so that it is only half-folded.

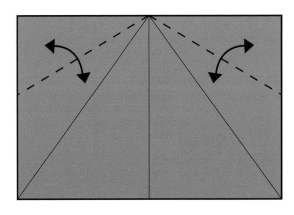

5. Fold in both layers from the center line as shown.

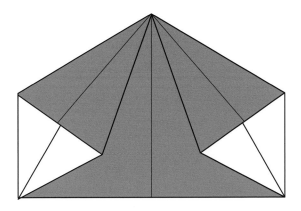

6. Open out and fold flat.

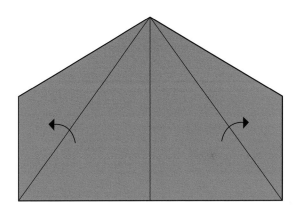

7. Fold the top layer of one side back along the diagonal. Fold in the top triangle over it. Match this on the lower layer. Repeat on the other side.

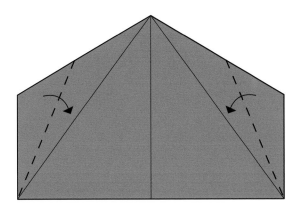

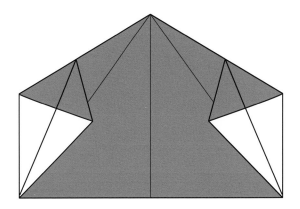

8. Fold out the top layer. Fold back the side edge as shown. Fold back the lower layer underneath.

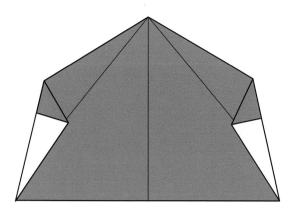

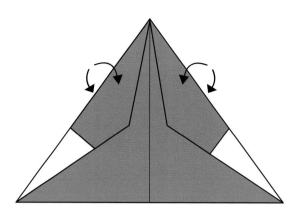

9. Repeat this process on the other side.

10. Fold the edges in, front and back.

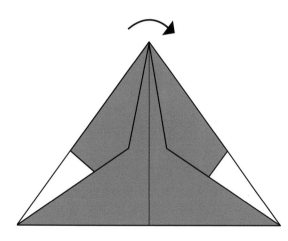

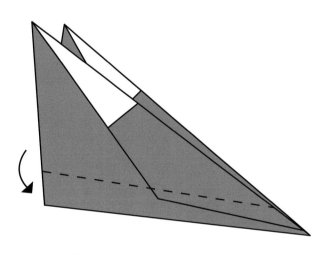

11. Fold the plane in half.

12. Fold down the wings, by folding from the nose along **the base of the wings**.

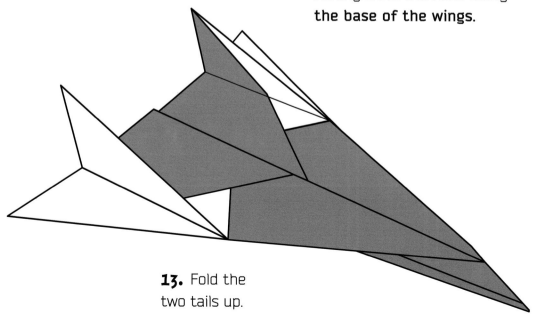

13. Fold the two tails up.

14. A paper clip holds the sides of the body together and balances the plane in flight.

Now fly!

Amazing Science

Planes fly because all the air particles beneath their wings lift them up. But the wings must keep moving more air under them to provide enough lift. They can do this because planes keep moving fast like this paper aircraft.

Candle Seesaw

You will need

One long, thin household candle

Two pins.

Old plate

2 feet (60 cm) thick nickel-plated wire

Shifting weight makes a candle rock back and forth . . .

Tools you will need
(see page 29)

✷ Pliers
✷ Side cutters
✷ Lighter

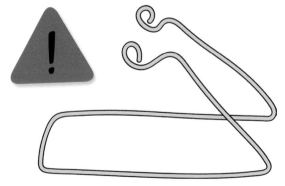

1. Trim the bottom off the candle leaving the wick exposed. The candle now has a wick at each end.

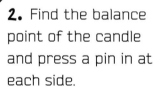

2. Find the balance point of the candle and press a pin in at each side.

3. Make this balance frame from the wire. It should be slightly wider than the candle.

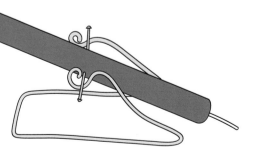

4. Drop the candle into position and place the seesaw on an old plate.

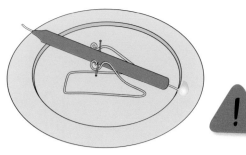

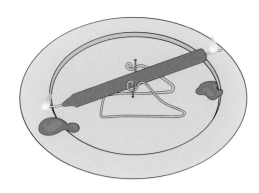

5. The candle will most likely be heavier on one side. Light it at the heavier end.

6. As the balance begins to change, light the other end of the candle

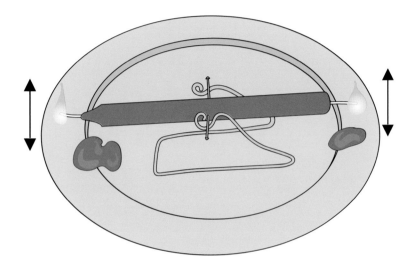

7. As the candle burns, the lower end will burn faster, making that end lighter. The candle will then tilt up. The process will repeat over and over.

It's a moving seesaw!

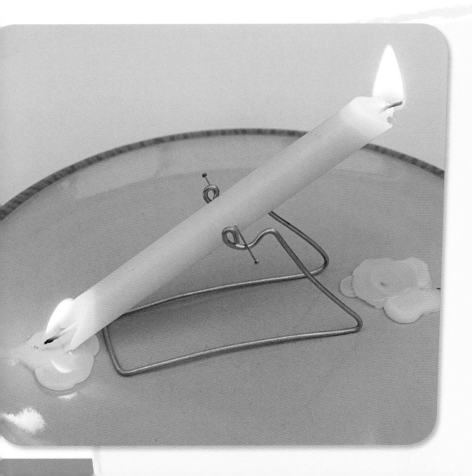

Amazing Science

A seesaw stays level when the riders are balanced in weight. But if one leans forward, they go up, because their weight has less leverage nearer the pivot. They lean back to go down again. The candle seesaws as either end becomes lighter as the wax melts and drips off the candle.

Soap-powered Boat

This little boat is propelled forward when soap touches the water it floats on. Water has high surface tension, while soap has low surface tension. They have net force when they interact known as the Marangoni effect (see Amazing Science opposite).

You Will need

Shallow tray

Liquid soap

Talcum powder (baby powder)

Thin, close celled craft foam, 4 x 3 in (10 x 7 cm)

Tools you Will need
(see page 29)

✷ Craft utility knife

1. To see the science at work, fill a shallow tray with water. Sprinkle a thin layer of talcum powder over the water.

2. Squeeze a single drop of liquid soap into the tray, A circle of clear water will quickly appear as the talcum powder is pushed back. The boat harnesses this amazing power.

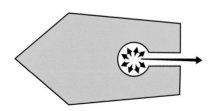

3. The boat has a circular hole in the body to take the drop of soap. The slot channels the soap out of the boat, powering it forward.

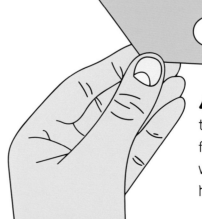

4. Use a craft knife to cut the boat shape from the craft foam, with a 1–inch (25 mm) hole and a slot.

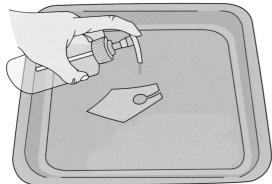

5. Float the boat on a tray of water and drip a drop of soap into the hole in the boat.

The boat shoots forward!

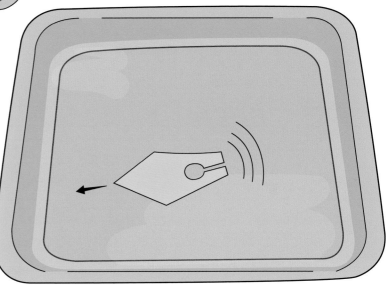

Amazing Science

Water molecules cling together at the surface, creating a skin held together by surface tension. A drop of soap breaks the tension so the boat moves. Small objects that are denser than water can also float due to surface tension.

Vortex

A vortex is a rotating fluid or gas. It may form a spiral as it loses energy, but a smoke ring is a kind of vortex that is doughnut-shaped and rotates around itself.

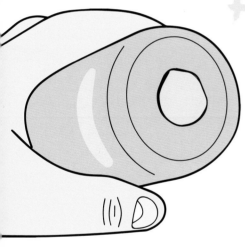

1. Cut a circular hole in the bottom of the plastic beaker.

2. Cut the top off a balloon.

3. Tie a knot in the stem of the balloon.

4. Stretch the balloon over the open end of the beaker.

46

5. Tape the edges of the balloon with gaffer tape.

6. Light an incense stick, and fill the beaker with smoke. Make sure you don't touch the balloon with the incense stick as it will burn through quickly!

7. Tap the balloon and a series of smoke rings will be created. The vortex moves slowly but the air in them spins fast. If you aim a vortex at a candle flame, you will be able to blow it out!

Amazing Science

When air is compressed (squeezed), its particles are packed together. So, the smoke particles in the jar are punched together when the balloon is pushed inwards and makes rotating smoke rings.

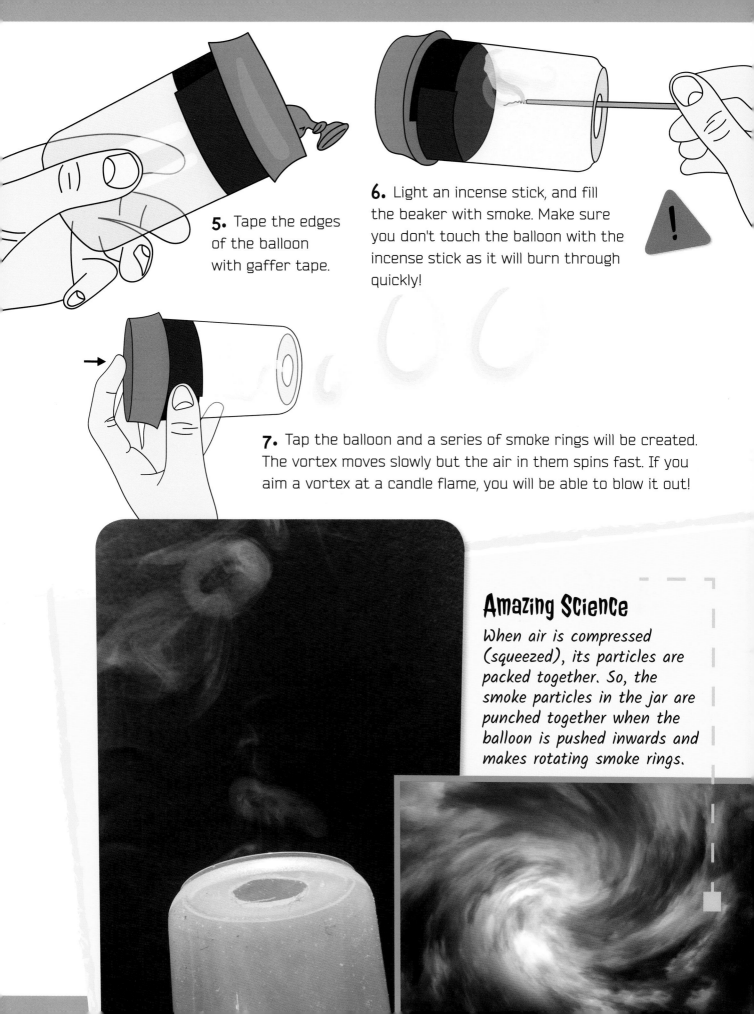

Light

Did you know that light is the fastest thing in the universe? In the time it takes you to read this sentence, light can travel to the Moon and back, in just 2.6 seconds. All light is tiny packets of energy called photons, shot out by atoms. Everything you see is just countless tiny photons hitting your eyes! Try out these fun projects to find out a few other things about light, too.

You'll see how light is reflected at particular angles when it strikes a mirror. You'll see how light is bent, or refracted, when it passes through glass or water. You'll also see how lenses in telescopes and microscopes use this refraction to magnify things. And there's much more—even seeing a rainbow tells you light is full of color!

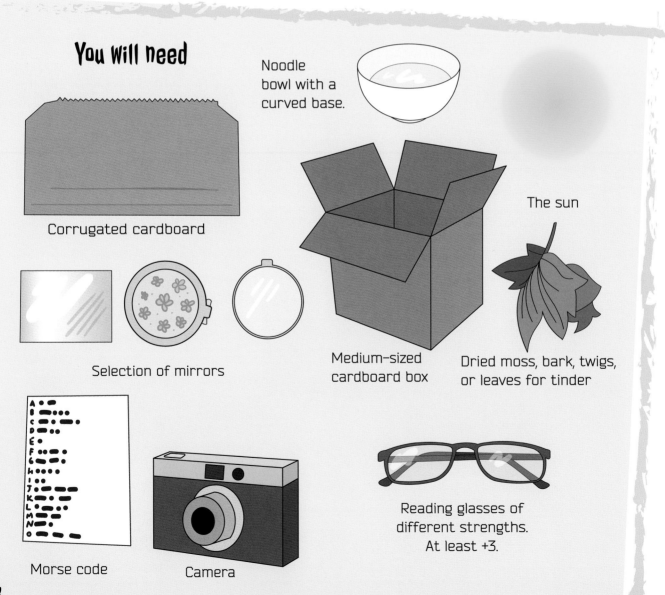

You will need

Noodle bowl with a curved base.

Corrugated cardboard

Selection of mirrors

Medium-sized cardboard box

The sun

Dried moss, bark, twigs, or leaves for tinder

Morse code

Camera

Reading glasses of different strengths. At least +3.

48

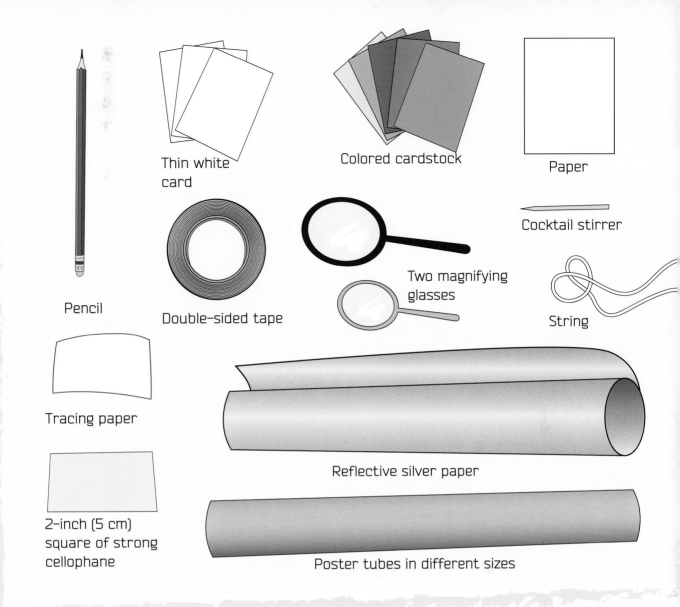

Pencil

Thin white card

Colored cardstock

Paper

Double-sided tape

Two magnifying glasses

Cocktail stirrer

String

Tracing paper

Reflective silver paper

2-inch (5 cm) square of strong cellophane

Poster tubes in different sizes

What tools will I need?

Craft utility knife

3.5-inch (90 mm) diameter tape roll

Gaffer tape (or duct tape)

Masking tape

Junior hacksaw

Kitchen scissors

Ruler

White glue

Clothespins

Periscope

A periscope is an optical device for changing your viewpoint. Probably the most famous use for the periscope is in a submarine. It allows the captain to see above the water level without having to break surface and reveal his position. Periscopes also allow small people to see what is going on when they are in the middle of a crowd. They are great for looking over tall walls, and you can even use them for watching the TV from behind the sofa!

You will need

Pencil

Poster tube, 2-inch (50 mm) diameter

Double-sided tape

Cheap compact mirror with two 2-inch (50 mm) mirrors

Scrap of corrugated cardboard

Tools you will need (see page 49)

★ White glue
★ Junior hacksaw
★ Masking tape

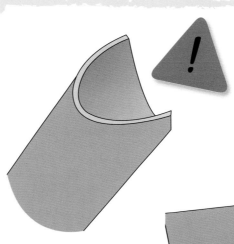

1. Saw the poster tube from the center of one end at a 45° angle, on both sides.

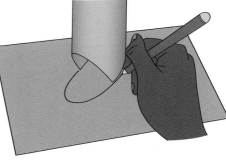

2. Repeat at the other end.

3. Draw halfway around one end of the tube on corrugated cardboard.

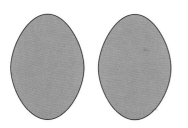

4. Complete the other half of your traced oval shape, then cut it out twice.

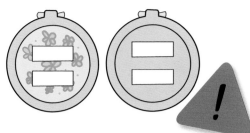

5. Split the mirror in two. Apply double-sided tape to the back of each one.

6. Stick the mirrors to the center of the card ovals.

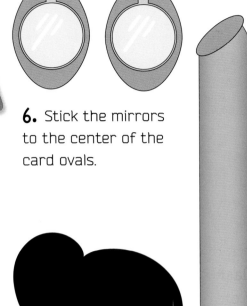

Your periscope is ready to use! Can you see inside that bird's nest in the park?

7. Glue one mirror card to one end and tape it down with masking tape until the glue dries.

8. Repeat at the other end, making sure the mirror is facing the other way. That's it!

Light enters and hits the top mirror.

The top mirror bounces the light onto the mirror below.

The lower mirror shows the view.

Amazing Science

When light hits a mirror at an angle, it bounces off at the same, but opposite, angle. Another mirror facing the first will show the original view. You can also see round corners with your periscope—just hold it sideways!

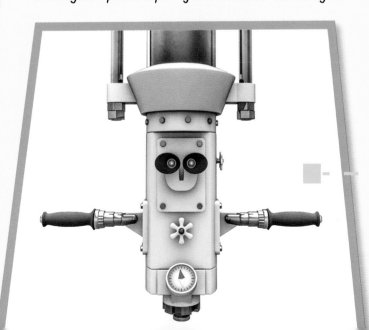

51

Camera Obscura

The camera obscura was the ancestor of the photographic camera. Here, a lens projects a picture upside-down onto a mirror, which flashes a corrected image onto tracing paper. There is also a shade on top to make the image clearer. Many years ago, artists used equipment like this to trace over a projected image. This was a starting point for their painting.

You Will need

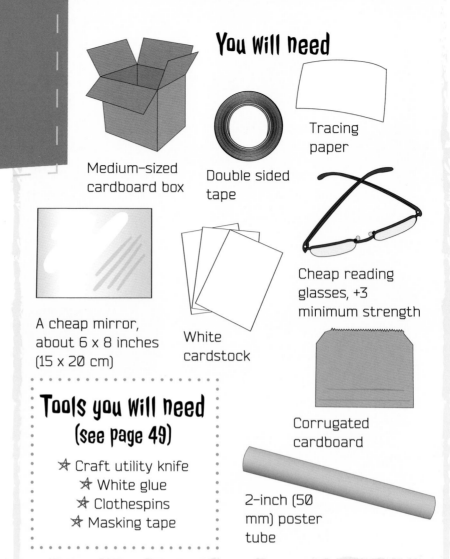

Medium-sized cardboard box

Double sided tape

Tracing paper

A cheap mirror, about 6 x 8 inches (15 x 20 cm)

White cardstock

Cheap reading glasses, +3 minimum strength

Corrugated cardboard

2-inch (50 mm) poster tube

Tools you Will need
(see page 49)

✳ Craft utility knife
✳ White glue
✳ Clothespins
✳ Masking tape

1. Pop out a lens from the glasses. Cut out a doughnut shape from corrugated cardboard, 3 inches (75 mm) across with a 1.5-inch (40 mm) diameter hole in the center.

2. Tape the lens over the hole with masking tape.

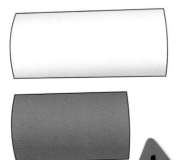

3. Cut a 4-inch (10 cm) section off the poster tube. Roll up an 8-inch (20 cm) length of white card and make a tube that fits inside the poster tube. The poster tube must be able to move back and forward on the white tube, like a telescope.

4. Glue the end of the poster tube to the lens doughnut card.

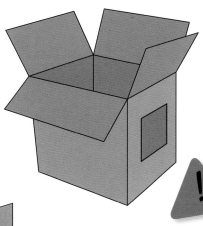

5. Cut a 4-inch square (10 cm) square hole in one side of your box with a craft knife.

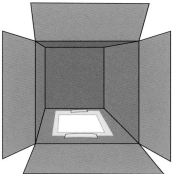

6. Tape the tracing paper over the hole on the inside with masking tape. Make sure it is taut. This is the screen and will be on the top.

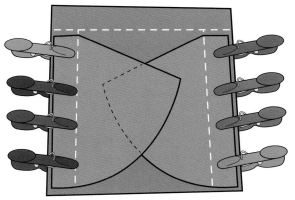

7. Make a shade for the top by cutting three pieces of corrugated cardboard as shown. One is square, the width of the box; and two have a slanted and a curved edge. Allow a 0.5-inch (15 mm) straight margin for each. Glue on the side pieces and hold in place with clothespins as it dries. Glue the square piece along its margin to the box to shade the screen.

8. Cut out a piece of corrugated cardboard that fits exactly across the diagonal of the box. Fix the mirror to it with double-sided tape.

9. Cut a hole for the lens tube in the front of the box and fit it in place. Close in the sides and tape them down to finish the camera obscura.

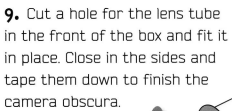

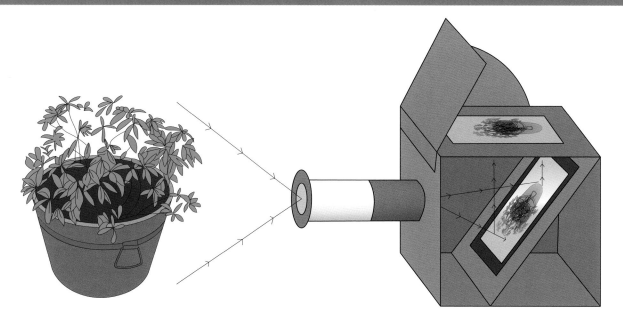

10. Point your lens at a brightly lit scene. Look down at the screen as you move the lens back and forward to focus the image there.

Amazing Science

When a light ray enters glass, it may be bent, or refracted. Lenses have curved surfaces that make all the rays bend towards the same point, or focus. Here, the lens and the mirror focus the light to project the scene on the tracing paper.

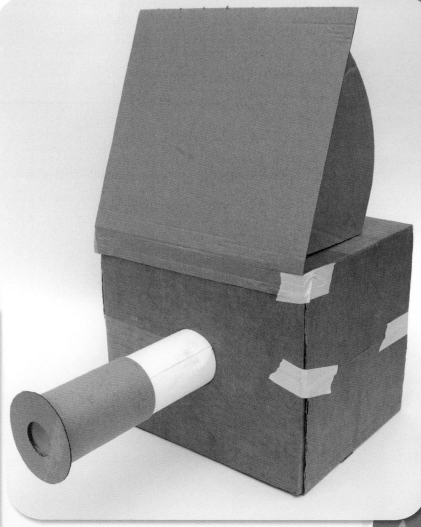

Kaleidoscope

2-inch (50 mm) poster tube

Corrugated cardboard

Cheap reading glasses, +2 strength

Reflective silver paper

2-inch (50 mm) double-sided tape

Tools you will need
(see page 49)

- ✴ Craft knife
- ✴ Gaffer tape
- ✴ Ruler
- ✴ White glue
- ✴ Kitchen scissors

The kaleidoscope is a 19th-century invention that uses a tube of three mirrors to create a colorful moving image. The kaleidoscope is so effective at creating swirling, changing colors that kaleidoscopic now means anything with quickly changing, bright colors.

1. Use a craft knife and ruler to cut the tube to roughly 7 inches (180 mm) in length. Cut three strips of corrugated cardboard, each 7 x 1.5 inches (180 x 43 mm).

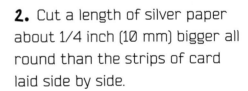

2. Cut a length of silver paper about 1/4 inch (10 mm) bigger all round than the strips of card laid side by side.

3. Apply 2-inch (50 mm) double-sided tape to the back of the card strips and trim it to fit. Peel off the backing.

4. Stick the card strips to the back of the silver paper so that they are touching each other. Trim the excess silver paper from around the edges.

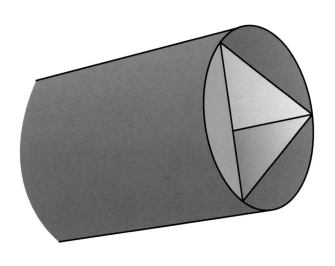

5. Fold along the edges of the card strips and fit the piece into the tube.

6. Pop out one of the lenses from the reading glasses. Cut a circle of card to cover the end of the poster tube and cut a circular hole in its center to match the width of the lens.

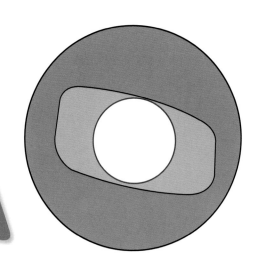

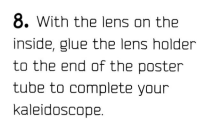

7. Tape the lens in place, making sure not to get tape over the hole.

8. With the lens on the inside, glue the lens holder to the end of the poster tube to complete your kaleidoscope.

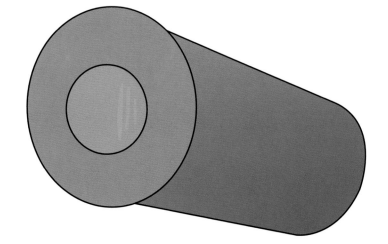

9. Point the open end of the kaleidoscope at colorful objects, such as flowers or bright pictures.

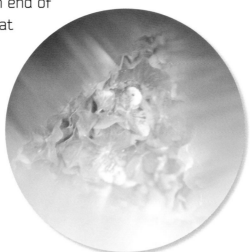

MARVEL AS the reflected COLORS SWIRL around When you move the kaleidoscope!

Amazing Science

The kaleidoscope was invented by English scientist Sir David Brewster in 1814. It uses three mirrors set at a slight angle to reflect each other in a perfectly symmetrical (matching) pattern. Colors swirl in different patterns as you view objects through the lens.

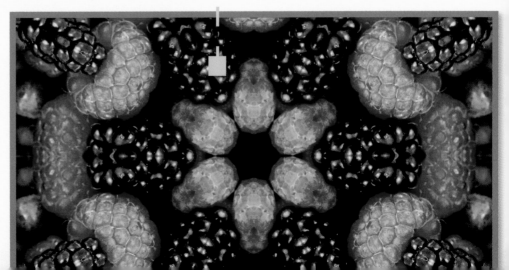

Heliograph

The sun

A small pocket mirror each

A copy of the Morse code x2

In the past, the heliograph was used to communicate over long distances. By flashing sunlight from one person to another, complicated messages could be sent at the speed of light. There are just a few problems with this: it has to be sunny, you must be able to see the person you are sending a message to, and it is s-l-o-w! But you can send a message several miles and it's difficult for anyone to eavesdrop.

Try it with a friend, using Morse code (below): short flashes for dots and long flashes for dashes.

Line up your friend with a target, and your signal will travel on to reach them too.

A ● ▬	U ● ● ▬
B ▬ ● ● ●	V ● ● ● ▬
C ▬ ● ▬ ●	W ● ▬ ▬
D ▬ ● ●	X ▬ ● ● ▬
E ●	Y ▬ ● ▬ ▬
F ● ● ▬ ●	Z ▬ ▬ ● ●
G ▬ ▬ ●	
H ● ● ● ●	
I ● ●	
J ● ▬ ▬ ▬	
K ▬ ● ▬	1 ● ▬ ▬ ▬ ▬
L ● ▬ ● ●	2 ● ● ▬ ▬ ▬
M ▬ ▬	3 ● ● ● ▬ ▬
N ▬ ●	4 ● ● ● ● ▬
O ▬ ▬ ▬	5 ● ● ● ● ●
P ● ▬ ▬ ●	6 ▬ ● ● ● ●
Q ▬ ▬ ● ▬	7 ▬ ▬ ● ● ●
R ● ▬ ●	8 ▬ ▬ ▬ ● ●
S ● ● ●	9 ▬ ▬ ▬ ▬ ●
T ▬	0 ▬ ▬ ▬ ▬ ▬

1. Choose an open space with the sun to one side of you when you face each other. Stand on either side of an object and line up your friend with the object.

2. Reflect the sunlight with your mirror onto the ground near you. You should see a bright spot the same shape as your mirror. Now shine it at the object.

3. Move it up just slightly to flash a beam at your friend. It will reach them because light travels in straight lines.

Ice Lens

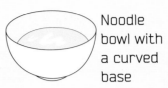
Can you start a camp fire using just ice? You can if the sun is shining!

1. When the boiled water is cool, pour it into the bowl to a depth of around 2 inches (5 cm).. Freeze it overnight to make your ice lens.

2. Warm the outside of the bowl in warm water and drop the lens into a gloved hand.

3. Arrange your tinder in a safe place outside. Use the ice lens to focus the sun's rays on the tinder until it starts to smoulder. Arrange some small twigs on top and make yourself a small camp fire!

Amazing Science

A convex, or outward-bulging, piece of clear ice acts like a lens, to focus the sun's rays together. The concentration of light can heat the tinder enough to start a fire. **Be sure to put out your mini campfire properly afterwards!**

Spinner

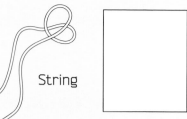

This spinner is an experiment in color mixing! As the disc spins fast, all the colors blur into one, revealing the average color.

You Will need

String

Paper

Corrugated cardboardboard

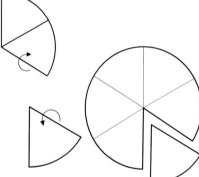

Colored cardstock

Tools you Will need (see page 49)

✯ 3.5-inch (90 mm) diameter tape roll
✯ White glue
✯ Kitchen scissors
✯ Pencil

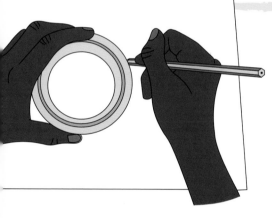

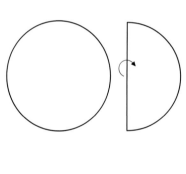

1. Trace the tape roll onto the paper. Cut out the circle, then fold it into six. Cut out one of the six segments. This will be your template.

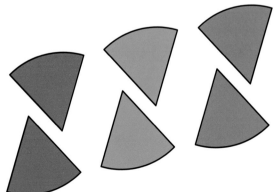

2. Cut out six segments of colored cardstock using your template as a guide.

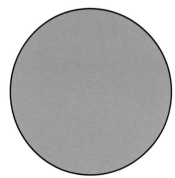

3. Cut out a corrugated cardboard disc using the same roll of tape as a template.

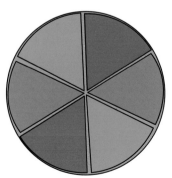

4. Glue the six segments onto the card as shown.

5. Make two holes off-center on the disc, and thread 30 inches (76 cm) of string through. Spin the disc by winding it up, then rhythmically pulling and releasing to speed it up.

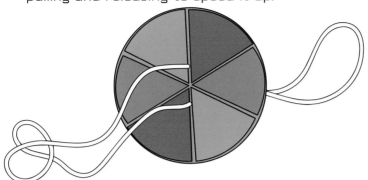

See if you can guess what color you will see before you start spinning. What happens if you mix yellow and red, black and white, blue and red? Are the color mixes the same as when you mix paint? What happens if you only add one slice of one color and five of another? What if you cover the disk in random circles of different colors!?

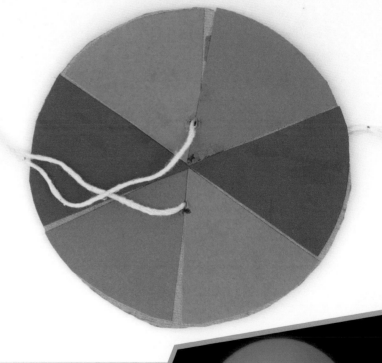

Amazing Science

When you spin a disc of colors, your eyes mix them together. If you combine just three basic, or primary, colors of light—red, blue and green—you get white. But colored cardstock is not the same as colored light, so here you end up with a brown color!

Stereoscopic Pictures

When you look at an object, you get two slightly different views of it, one to each eye. Your brain merges the picture together to reveal it in 3D! You can also fool your brain by recreating two different views in photographs. These paired pictures can be seen in 3D with the viewer from p. 64.

You will need

Camera

Thin white card

...and a printer and paper

Tools you will need (see page 49)

✴ White glue

1. For your pictures, choose a subject with good front-to-back depth. Complex, intricate objects, such as bushes or trees, also work well. Check that the lighting is constant and the object is stationary.

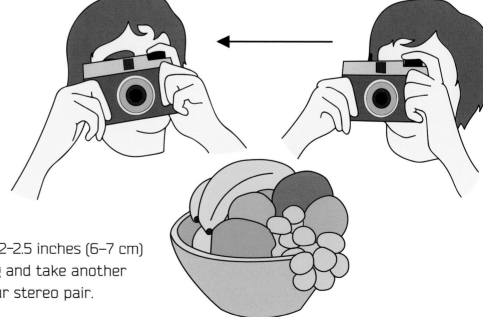

2. Take a photograph. Move 2–2.5 inches (6–7 cm) to your right without turning and take another photograph. These will be your stereo pair.

3. Print out both pictures so that they are roughly 2 inches (55 mm) wide. This is the best fit for the viewer in the next project.

4. Glue both pictures to a piece of card with a very small gap between them. The first picture goes on the left, the second on the right.

Try other subjects such as still life or outdoor plants...

Find out how to see these pictures in stereo on pages 64 and 65...

StereoViewer

You will need

A simple viewer allows you to see the 3D effect of the stereoscopic pictures you made on p. 62.

Tools you will need (see page 49)

✴ Craft utility knife
✴ Gaffer tape
✴ White glue
✴ Clothespins

Corrugated cardboard

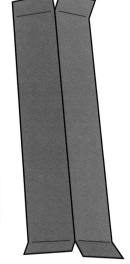
Strong reading glasses, +3 strength

1. Carefully pop the lenses out of the reading glasses.

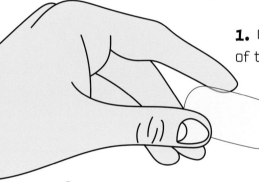

A 5.5 x 3 inches (140 x 80mm)

C 7.75 x 1.5 inches (200 x 40mm)

2. Cut out the three pieces A, B, and C as shown. Cut holes in B slightly smaller than the lenses, with the centers 3 inches (80 mm) apart. On C, mark and score tab and center lines. Make notches and fold along the score lines.

B

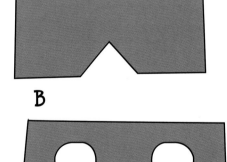

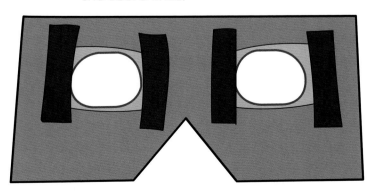

3. Tape the lenses in position with gaffer tape.

4. Assemble the three parts, fixing the tabs with white glue. Use clothespins to hold them together until the glue has dried.

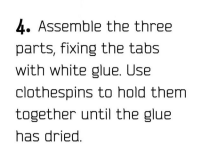

5. Cut out a small shelf from cardboard to fit on the back plate. Sit your stereoscopic pictures in place and view them through the lenses. Allow your eyes to relax and a 3D image will appear!

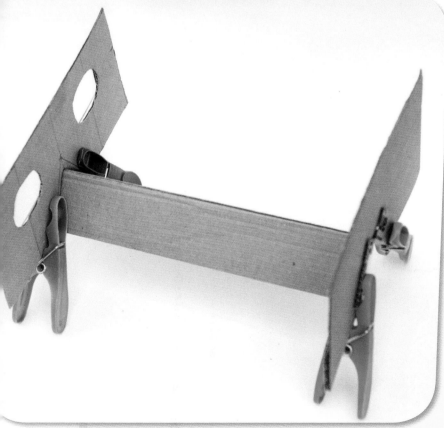

Amazing Science

The small distance between your eyes means each receives a slightly different view of the world. These two different views are transmitted to the brain, which merges them to give the impression of depth and solidity.

Telescope

A single lens can magnify things close by. A telescope allows you to see far away, because it has at least two lenses, or curved mirrors. Dutchman Hans Lippershey, who made magnifiers, is the likely inventor of the telescope, in 1608.

You Will need

Pencil

White card

Corrugated cardboard

Two magnifying glasses: one with a wide lens (e.g. 4 inches/75 mm) at 4x magnification; and one with a small lens (e.g. 1 inch/30 mm) at 20x magnification

A poster tube roughly the same diameter as the large lens

Tools you Will need
(see page 49)

✷ White glue
✷ Gaffer tape
✷ Ruler
✷ Craft utility knife

1. Find the focal length of the two lenses. Hold the weaker lens up to focus a clear image from outside onto your wall. Measure the distance from the lens to the wall.

2. Repeat with the more powerful lens. The focal length will be much shorter.

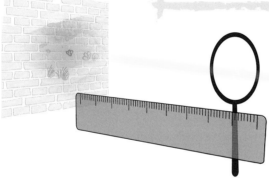

3. Add the two focal lengths together (example above: 16 cm + 2 cm = 18 cm). Your poster tube should be a couple of cm shorter than the combined focal length.

4. Fit the large lens to the end of the poster tube with glue or tape.

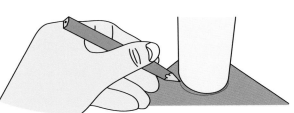

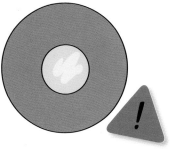

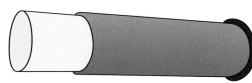

5. Roll up an 8-inch (20 cm) length of thin white card so that it will just fit inside the tube. Draw round the end on a piece of corrugated cardboard.

6. Cut out the card circle. Cut out a hole in the center and tape the smaller lens over the hole.

7. Fit the inner tube into the outer tube.

8. Tape or glue the small lens over the end of the inner tube. This tube should be able to move back and forwards in the outer tube. Do this to focus your image. Close objects will need a longer tube, distant objects a shorter tube.

9. Look through your telescope. Notice that the image is inverted! This is always the case with this type of telescope.

Don't look at the sun!

Amazing Science

The larger lens in a telescope brings light rays from the distance together, and the smaller one magnifies the image enough for you to see it.

Matter

Matter is everything in the universe that's not just empty space. In fact, most of the universe is empty space, but there's still an awful lot of matter—enough to make a solid ball stretching all the way to the nearest star and back!

It comes in three main forms: solid, liquid, and gas. These are called states of matter and seem very different, but matter can actually switch from one state to the other and back if the temperature and pressure are right. Your body is made from a mix of all three states of matter.

Here you'll learn how to make giant bubbles, flour that bounces, a superpowered fountain and much more. Matter matters!

You will need

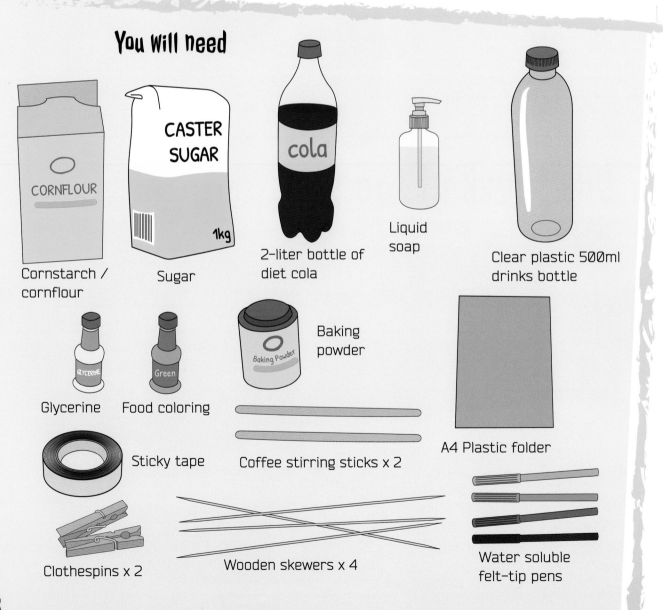

Cornstarch / cornflour

Sugar

2-liter bottle of diet cola

Liquid soap

Clear plastic 500ml drinks bottle

Glycerine

Food coloring

Baking powder

A4 Plastic folder

Sticky tape

Coffee stirring sticks x 2

Clothespins x 2

Wooden skewers x 4

Water soluble felt-tip pens

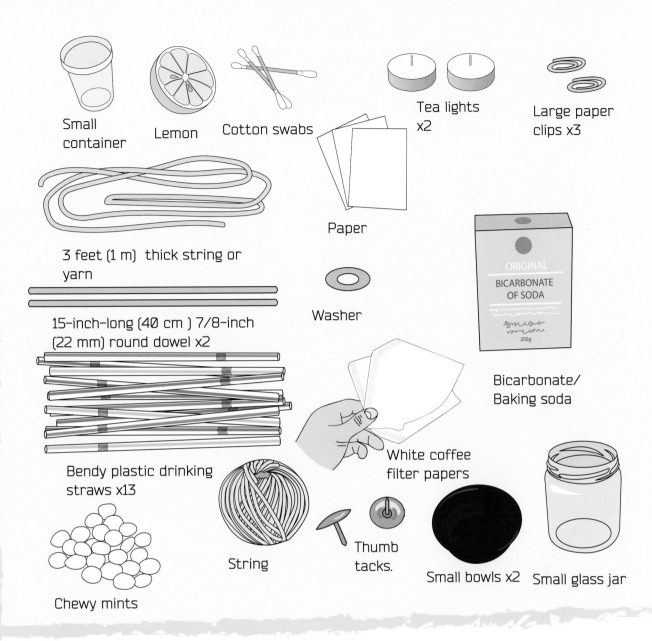

Small container

Lemon

Cotton swabs

Tea lights x2

Large paper clips x3

Paper

3 feet (1 m) thick string or yarn

Washer

ORIGINAL
BICARBONATE
OF SODA

200g

Bicarbonate/ Baking soda

15-inch-long (40 cm) 7/8-inch (22 mm) round dowel x2

Bendy plastic drinking straws x13

White coffee filter papers

String

Thumb tacks.

Small bowls x2

Small glass jar

Chewy mints

What tools will I need?

Saucepan

Pliers

Scissors

Shallow tray

Stapler

Gaffer tape (or duct tape)

Large jug

Cup

Butter knife

Measuring spoons

Pencil

Tea spoons

Cartesian Diver

This clever toy, invented by French thinker René Descartes, features a tiny diving tube in a bottle. The diver sinks when the bottle is squeezed. The pressure from your hand makes it move—relax your hand and up it pops!

You will need

Tea light

Thumb tacks x 2

Plastic drinking straw

Clear plastic 500ml drinks bottle

Tools you will need
(see page 69)

✭ Butter knife ✭ Scissors

Do not place fingers, clothing or any other materials near the flame. Extinguish the flame immediately upon completing the experiment.

1. Heat the end of the straw so that it just starts to melt.

2. Squash the end of the straw down with a blunt knife to seal it.

3. Trim the straw at the other end with scissors to roughly 1.5 to 2 inches (4–5 cm) in length.

4. Push a thumb tack in from each side of the straw at the open end. These act as weights so that the straw floats upright.

5. Fill the bottle with water right up to the top.

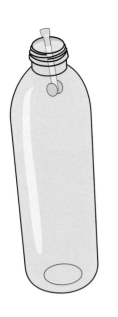

6. Drop the diver into the water. A few millimeters of the straw should be above the surface of the water. If the diver sticks out a long way, shorten the straw. If it sinks straight away, start again with a longer section of straw.

7. Fit the lid on the bottle and screw it down tight.

Squeeze the bottle to control the diver!

Bubble Mix

This bubble recipe only needs ingredients from the kitchen cupboard. The cornstarch / cornflour and glycerine adds to its strength. Prepare it for the next two experiments, which show how water can be made to hold pockets of air—quite big ones, too!

Baking powder

Glycerine

Cornstarch / cornflour

1/2 cup liquid dish soap

Tools you will need (see page 69)
✷ Cup ✷ Measuring spoons ✷ Large jug

1. Add two tablespoons of cornstarch / cornflour to a cup.

2. Add water, a little at a time, and stir it in until the cup is full.

3. Add the mixture to a large jug, then **add two more cups of water.**

4. Measure out **half a cup** of liquid soap..

5. Add the detergent to the mix.

6. Add a **tablespoon** of glycerine.

7. Add a **teaspoon** of baking powder.

8. Mix thoroughly but gently. The bubble mix works best when not covered in a foam!

Amazing Science

When water is mixed with soap, the soap weakens its surface tension. Surface tension is the attraction between water molecules, which normally pull the water together into a droplet. Air can then move in to form a bubble.

Big Bubbles

Using the bubble mix recipe from pp.72-73, you can take a giant step forward in bubble-making with this experiment.

You will need

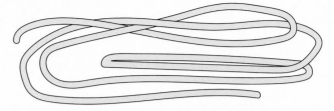

3-foot-long (1-m) thick string or yarn

15-inch-long (40 cm) 7/8-inch (22 mm) round dowel x2

Tools you will need
(see page 69)

⭐Pliers

Gaffer tape

Large paper clips x2

1. Use pliers to help you unfold the paper clips, and fold them round into a U shape.

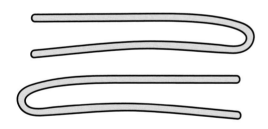

2. Hold a paper clip over the end of each stick to make a loop, and tape it in place.

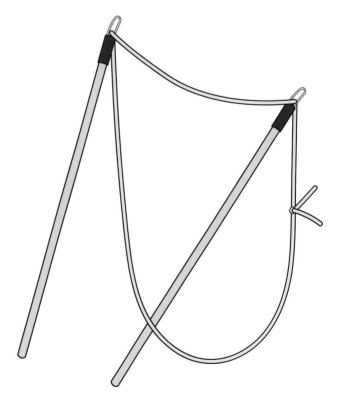

3. Thread the string through the loops at the end of the sticks. Tie the ends to make a loop.

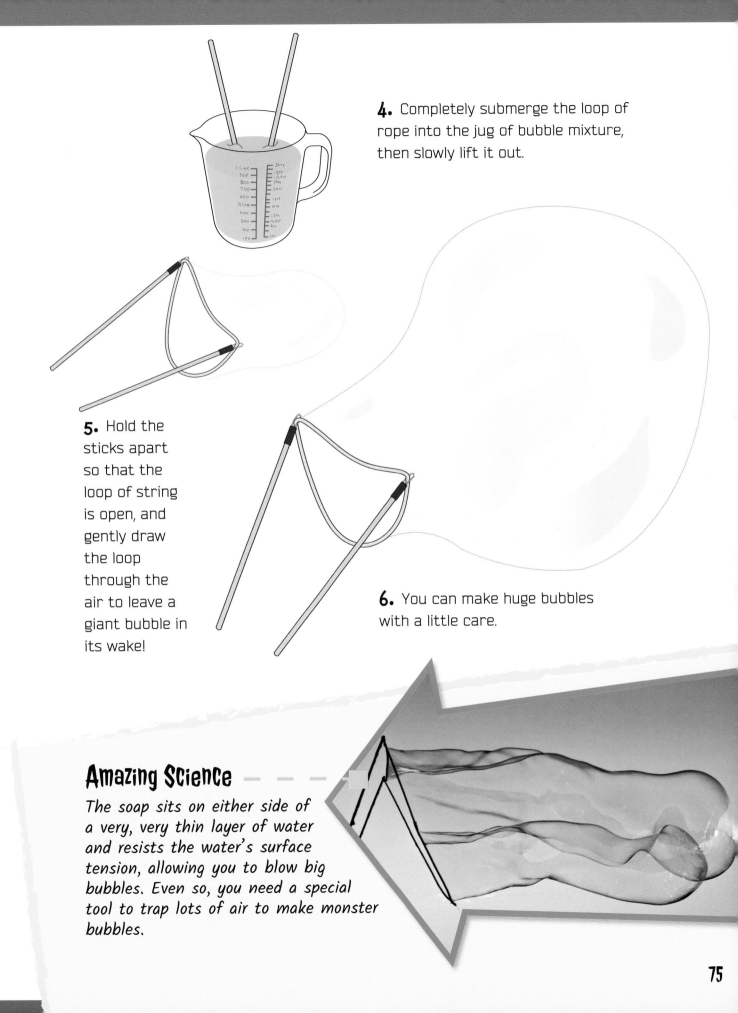

4. Completely submerge the loop of rope into the jug of bubble mixture, then slowly lift it out.

5. Hold the sticks apart so that the loop of string is open, and gently draw the loop through the air to leave a giant bubble in its wake!

6. You can make huge bubbles with a little care.

Amazing Science

The soap sits on either side of a very, very thin layer of water and resists the water's surface tension, allowing you to blow big bubbles. Even so, you need a special tool to trap lots of air to make monster bubbles.

Bubble Cube

Want a change from round bubbles? Again using the mix from pp.72-73, this time construct a cube frame to make a big bubble that mirrors its straight-sided shape.

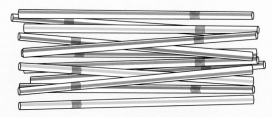
1. Bend a straw to a 90° angle.

2. Squidge up the short end so it will fit into another straw.

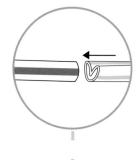

3. Fit four straws together like this to make a square.

4. Repeat the process to make a second square.

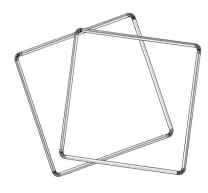

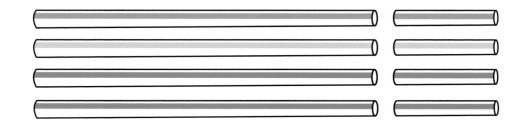

5. Cut the bendy sections off four more straws and discard them.

6. Push a wooden skewer through the corner of one of the squares. **BEWARE OF THE SHARP ENDS..**

7. Repeat on all the other corners. Push them up to be even with the straw square.

8. Slip the four cut-off straws over the skewers.

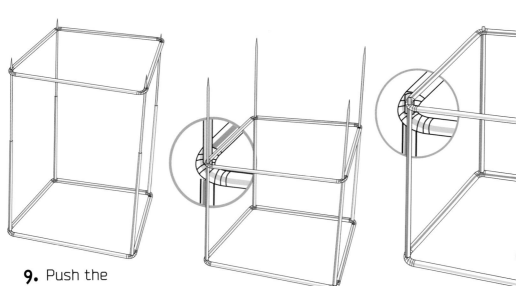

9. Push the second square down over the skewers.

10. Keep pushing the square down till it rests on the four upright straws.

11. Trim off the ends of the skewers with scissors. .

12. Pour bubble mix into a tray. Dip the cube into the mix and rotate it so that each face is immersed. Lift the cube out.

13. A cube-shaped bubble will be suspended between the faces. You may need to give it a couple of tries!

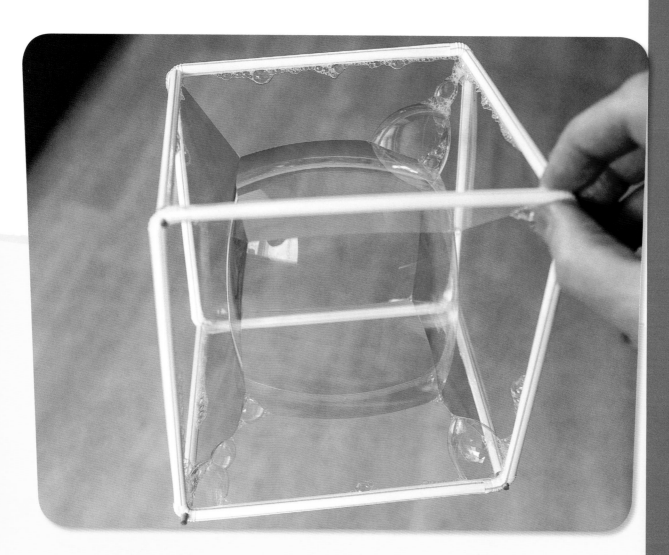

Amazing Science

Floating bubbles are naturally round because that shape keeps them most stable—the surface area is the smallest (and strongest) for enclosing the maximum amount of air. But bubbles can also mirror geometric structures like this cube shape, which allows for a minimal surface area.

Cornstarch / Cornflour Slime

Small bowls x2

Water

CORNFLOUR

Cornstarch / cornflour

Tools you Will need (see page 69)

✮Teaspoon
✮Measuring spoon

Cornstarch / cornflour is a fascinating material. When mixed with water in the correct proportions, it becomes what is known as a non-Newtonian fluid. This has some really weird properties!

1. Add **three tablespoons** of cornstarch / cornflour to one bowl. Add water a little at a time, mixing it gently until it becomes a thick paste.

2. Time to experiment! Pour the mix from one bowl to another. It will flow smoothly just like any normal liquid.

3. Now try stirring it with a spoon. If you stir it slowly, it will be just like any other liquid, but the faster you try to stir it, the thicker and harder the mix becomes. If you move your spoon through the mix really fast, it becomes a solid and will even crack and break! Amazing!

Amazing Science

Most liquids splash or flow away if you hit them. But not cornstarch slime. It is a non-Newtonian fluid, so it can behave like a liquid or a solid. It locks solid when you hit it hard and only flows if you push gently. That's because when you hit it, the water in the slime rushes away, leaving solid cornstarch.

Bouncy Ball

Here's another way to transform cornstarch/cornflour—this time into a squishy object. Just add water and then cook up your ball! Remember to keep your spoonfuls consistent.

You will need

Food coloring

Small bowl

Water

CORNFLOUR

Cornstarch / cornflour

Tools you will need
(see page 69)

✶ Measuring spoons
✶ Microwave

1. Mix **three tablespoons** of cornstarch / cornflour and **a tablespoon** of water in a bowl. You may need a little extra water.

2. Add a few drops of food coloring and mix it in.

3. Microwave the mixture for **20 seconds**, then mix in another teaspoon of water.

4. When cool enough, roll the mixture into a ball between your palms.

5. Microwave the ball for an additional **15 seconds**

6. Let the ball cool completely, then give it a try!

Amazing Science

Not all solid substances are rigid. Some are elastic. They might stretch or squeeze under pressure but bounce back to their original shape. A rubber ball squishes out of shape when it hits the ground, then shoots itself up in the air as it regains its shape.

Separating Colors

A solution is a liquid with substances dissolved in it. The technique for separating out the colors in solutions is called chromatography. It is used here to find out what colors make up the inks in felt-tip pens. Dark colored pens work best!

White coffee filter papers

Water soluble felt tip pens

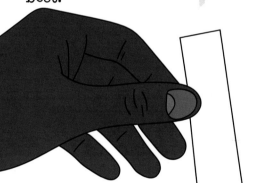

Coffee stirring stick

You will need

Clothespins x2

Tools you will need
(see page 69)

✭ Shallow tray
✭ Scissors
✭ Stapler

1. Cut four thin strips from the coffee filter, all about 3 inches (70 mm) long.

2. Fold over the ends of the strips and staple them down, making a loop that the coffee stirrer fits through.

3. Choose four water-soluble felt-tip pens for your investigation. Draw a line across one paper strip with a pen, roughly 0.5 inches (15 mm) from the end of the strip.

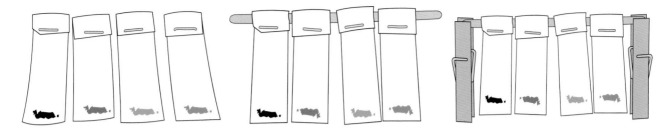

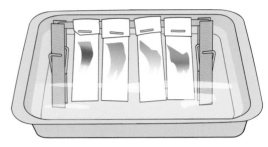

4. Prepare a few different colors in the same way.

5. Thread the coffee stirrer through the ends of the strips.

6. Make a frame with the two clothespins as shown.

7. Stand the frame in a shallow tray and add water just to reach the bottom of the strips.

8. As the water soaks its way up the strips, it pulls the inks with it. Some colors move higher up the strips than others, which causes them to separate.

Amazing Science

The inks separate into their colors because they behave differently in contact with water. Some flow more easily than others and move further up the paper.

Growing Crystals

CASTER SUGAR

1kg

Bag of sugar

Small glass jar

String

Crystals are both fascinating and beautiful! You can grow your own with just a few household items. Here, we grow sugar crystals, but you can also try using salt or baking powder in the same way.

Mug of water for measuring

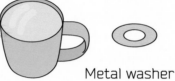

Metal washer

Coffee stirrer

Tools you Will need
(see page 69)

✱ Saucepan ✱ Spoon

Food coloring

Orange

1. Tie the washer to one end of a length of string. Tie the other end to the coffee stirrer.

2. Lay the stick across the jar. Adjust the length of the string so that the washer hangs just above the bottom of the jar. Set aside.

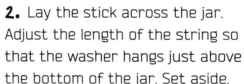

3. Pour a mug of water into a pan and boil.. Add sugar to the water, one spoonful at a time. Stir the water until the sugar is completely dissolved.

4. Keep adding sugar until no more will dissolve. This is known as a saturated solution, and it will be quite thick and syrupy. If you want colored crystals, add a few drops of food coloring.

5. Let the liquid cool, then pour it into the jar.

7. Now leave it! Come back in a week and you'll find beautiful crystals have formed on the string.

6. Dangle your string in the solution.

Amazing Science

Everything is made of tiny particles called atoms. Atoms form molecules, and in a crystal these have regular geometric shapes. Crystals grow gradually as molecules join. In a crystal, the joined atoms form regular, geometric shapes. Here, as water evaporates from the saturated sugar-water solution, sugar molecules are left behind. They collect on the string to form crystals..

Invisible Ink

You will need

Pencil

Tea light

Send secret messages to your spy friends, using your very own invisible ink.

Small container

Lemon

Cotton buds

Paper

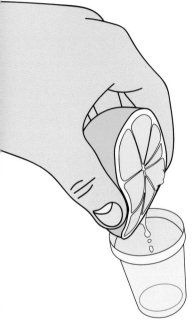

1. Squeeze some lemon juice into the container.

2. Mark out a rectangle in pencil on the paper for your message. The ink really is invisible, and this will show you where you've written.

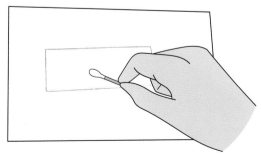

4. Write your message in lemon juice inside the rectangle. Keep dipping the cotton bud in the lemon juice to keep it "charged."

3. Dip a cotton bud in the lemon juice.

5. Let the message dry completely.

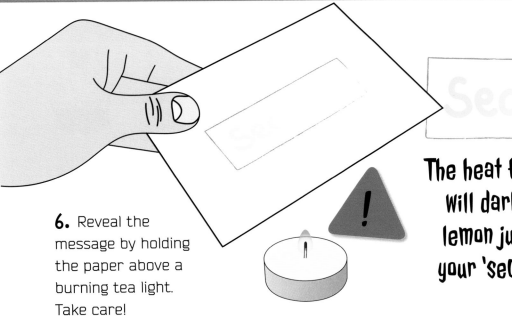

6. Reveal the message by holding the paper above a burning tea light. Take care!

The heat from the candle will darken the dried lemon juice, revealing your 'secret' message!

Amazing Science

Normally lemon juice is almost transparent. But if you heat it, the juice reacts with oxygen in the air and turns brown. This is called oxidation. It is an example of a chemical reaction: the change that occurs in chemicals when they meet. Rust is the oxidation of iron when it meets air and water, as you can see on this can to the right.

Spring Fountain

A remote-controlled fountain made from effervescent diet cola and chewy mints really packs a pop!

You will need

Chewy mints

Large paper clip

10 feet (3 m) string

2-liter bottle of diet cola

A4 plastic folder

Sticky tape

Tools you will need
(see page 69)

✭ Pliers ✭ Scissors

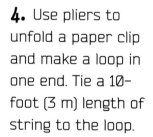

1. Cut one side from the plastic wallet and roll it into a tube.

2. Make sure it will fit tightly in the neck of the bottle. Secure with a couple of pieces of sticky tape.

3. Make a small hole on either side of the tube with the point of a pair of scissors.

4. Use pliers to unfold a paper clip and make a loop in one end. Tie a 10-foot (3 m) length of string to the loop.

5. Fit the pin through the holes in the plastic tube. This will be your release mechanism to trigger the reaction!

6. Remove the tube, keeping the pin in place, and fill it with chewy mints from the top.

88

7. Now go outside!

Open the bottle, and fit the tube in the neck. Stand at a safe distance holding the end of the string.

3...2...1...
...pull the string!

8. The mints are released into the cola — and whoosh! The drink shoots out of the bottle in a fizzy fountain!

Amazing Science

The drink is bubbly because it is full of carbon dioxide gas. The mints have tiny dimples on their surface which make bubbles form fast. When the mints are dropped in with the soda all at once, they create an explosive effect..

✻ Some animals have the magnetic substance magnetite in their bodies. Homing pigeons have it in their beaks and it may help them to navigate.

✻ Magnets can lift cars, but the world's most powerful magnet, at Los Alamos Laboratory in New Mexico, USA, is about 50 times more powerful than those magnets.

✻ The electricity used in homes alternates or switches direction about 50 times a second.

✻ Electricity travels at 95% the speed of light through a copper wire.

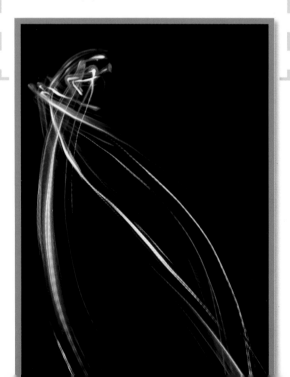

✻ A bolt of lightning can measure up to 3,000,000 volts, reach 54,000°F (30,000°C) and lasts a fraction of a second.

✻ An electric eel can give a shock of 500 volts.

✶ The Hubble Space Telescope, launched in 1990, has an 8-ft mirror for collecting available light.

✶ Robert Goddard built the first rocket in 1926. It climbed 40 ft (12 m) in 2.5 seconds.

✶ British inventor Christopher Cockerell had to battle to get his hovercraft design taken seriously. The Navy called it a plane not a boat, the Air Force called it a boat not a plane. It made a successful test-crossing of the English Channel in 1959, and then it really took off in the 1960s.

In 1995, American Bob Windt set a record of 85.38 mph (137.4 km/h) racing his hovercraft on Portugal's River Douro.

✶ A rocket has to travel at about 20 times the speed of sound to reach space from Earth. That's 4.9 mps (7.9 km/s). Many have done so, including the US's Atlas V, used to put satellites in orbit. On March 1, 2017, it accomplished its 70th mission.

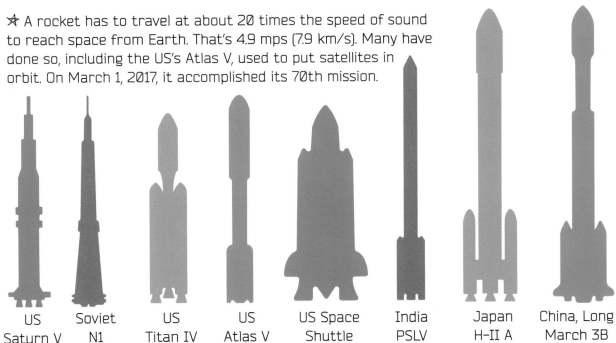

US Saturn V Soviet N1 US Titan IV US Atlas V US Space Shuttle India PSLV Japan H-II A China, Long March 3B

Not to scale

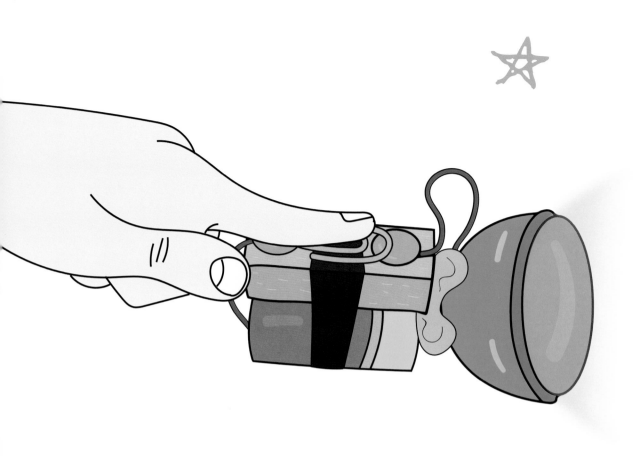

The Author

Rob Ives is a former maths and science teacher, now a designer and paper engineer living in Cumbria, UK. He creates science- and project-based children's books, including *Paper Models that Rock!* and *Paper Automata*. He specializes in character-based paper animations and all kinds of fun and fascinating science projects, and he often visits schools to talk about design technology and demonstrate his models.

The Illustrator

Eva Sassin is a freelance illustrator born in London, UK. She has always loved illustrating, whether it be scary, fun monsters or cute, sparkly fairies. She carries a sketchbook everywhere, but she has even drawn on the back of receipts if she's forgotten it! In her free time, she travels around London to visit exhibitions and small cafés where she enjoys sketching up new ideas and characters. She is also a massive film buff!

INDEX

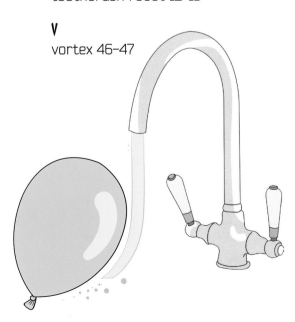

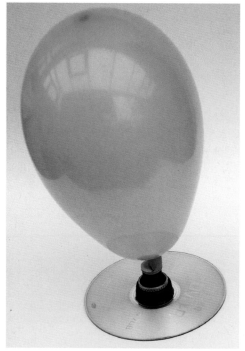